James McNair's
CHEESE
Cookbook

James McNair's
CHEESE
Cookbook

Photography by Patricia Brabant
Chronicle Books · San Francisco

Printed in Japan

Library of Congress
Cataloging-in-Publication Data
McNair, James K.
(Cheese cookbook)
James McNair's Cheese Cookbook
Bibliography: p.
Includes index.
1. Cookery (Cheese)
2. Cheese.
I. Title
TX759.M38 1986 641.6'73 86-14715
ISBN 0-87701-705-0
ISBN 0-87701-653-4 (pbk.)

Distributed in Canada by
Raincoast Books
112 East Third Avenue
Vancouver, British Columbia V5T 1C8

10 9 8 7 6 5 4 3 2 1

Chronicle Books
275 Fifth Street
San Francisco, California 94103

Produced by The Rockpile Press, San Francisco and Lake Tahoe

Art direction, photographic and food styling, and book design by James McNair

Editorial production assistance by Lin Cotton

Photography assistance by Louis Block

Typography and mechanical production by Cleve Gallat, Peter Linato, and Don Kruse of CTA Graphics

To my mother Lucille McNair with thanks for those pimiento-cheese sandwiches, for encouraging my early interest in cooking, and for her continued love and support through the years.

All dinnerware has been graciously provided from the collection of San Francisco's Dishes Delmar.

CONTENTS

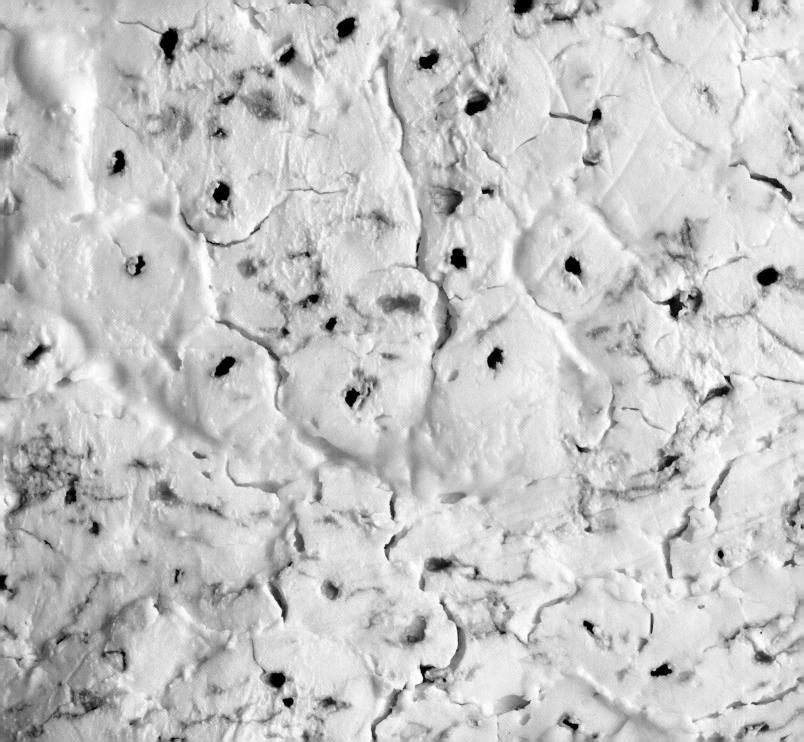

INTRODUCTION

When I was growing up in small-town Louisiana of the forties and fifties, cheese, like everything else, meant American, or occasionally Cheddar or Swiss, though I doubt that the "Swiss" that was available had ever seen the Alps.

Cheese was something we had for breakfast at my grandmother's house in Mississippi, along with country ham, eggs, cloud-light white biscuits, homemade jams and jellies, and garden-ripe tomatoes. I always found Cheddar slices for breakfast quite exotic, for back in our own home my mother, who's always been a marvelous southern cook, used cheese mainly to top casseroles.

As a youngster my favorite picnic fare included icy watermelons and sandwiches filled with a spread of pimiento cheese. My mother would grate some sort of yellow-orange cheese and then mix it with minced canned pimiento, mayonnaise, or rather Miracle Whip, and, of course, a bit of sugar, before generously slathering it on crust-trimmed white bread. I couldn't resist including a grown-up version of this childhood summer memory in these pages.

Some people who ate at Bill's Cafe ordered cheese on their hamburgers, but I'd only eat meat and mayonnaise on mine. Finally I was converted to cheeseburgers at Minnie and Shorty's drive-in and they became standard fare through all those years in Jonesville. I'd love one right now.

Parmesan was something out of a green box to sprinkle on the meat balls and spaghetti that I often ordered when our family ate out in nearby Natchez. My daddy wouldn't touch the stuff; he said it smelled like dirty feet and tasted like sawdust. He's always been a wise man.

Oh yes, there was always Cream cheese, usually as an ingredient in "cherry-o-cheese" pies made with the magic of condensed milk, or in congealed "salads," which were wonderfully creamy and would have been marvelous desserts but were always served along with the meal.

It wasn't until I moved to New York that I discovered that Cream cheese was made to spread on bagels or turn into cheesecakes. Living only a few blocks from Zabar's, the world-famous food emporium that's a bit of heaven on earth, I was exposed to a whole world of cheese tastes and textures about which I'd never even dreamed. I ate my way through them all, slowly acquiring a taste for stronger or riper flavors. I discovered real Parmigiano Reggiano, which remains my very favorite cheese; when freshly cut and eaten out of hand, it's better than candy. Sometimes I cook pasta merely as an excuse to eat Parmigiano. There was nutty Emmentaler or Jarlsberg, oozing Bries and Camemberts that took some getting accustomed to, herbal or peppery Boursin, real Cheddar from Vermont or England, and caramellike goat's milk Gjetost.

Many people, including the author, think of Gorgonzola as the best of the blue-veined cheese.

A decade later in San Francisco, I got involved with cheese in a way that almost gave me my fill of it. Lin Cotton and I opened the Twin Peaks Grocery, which we soon renamed Twin Peaks Gourmet in an attempt to dissuade people from stopping in vain for a pack of cigarettes. There, under the tutelage of Phil Quattrociocchi, of San Francisco International Cheese Imports, I learned a lot about cheeses, especially how fragile many were and how many chunks or whole ones had to be discarded in order to maintain absolute freshness and quality. Virginia and Buster, our dogs, got very fat from overindulging in triple-crèmes. After that brief, yet much too long, retailing experience, cheese sellers of quality have my admiration.

Today, it's hard to keep up with all the new cheeses that appear in the markets. Sometimes it seems like a new status cheese is introduced every few weeks, as importers find new ways of shipping very fragile cheeses from out-of-the-way European villages. And by becoming a nation of cheese connoisseurs, we've encouraged a whole new breed of high-quality cheese makers within our own shores.

This book is a collection of recipes featuring cheeses and of ideas for using cheeses in special presentations. You'll discover new ways to include cheese in your menus, as well as be reminded of forgotten favorites. Preceding the recipes are a few guidelines, including a directory of international cheeses and information on buying and storing them.

In keeping with the current trend toward interchanging meal courses, the recipes are divided into three major categories:

STARTERS, tasty morsels to whet the appetite or serve as light meals;

HEARTY FARE, a group of dishes that can star at family meals or entertainments, or be served in smaller portions for snacks or starters; and

ENDINGS, a look at the cheese course and a few luscious cheese sweets.

The tableware photographed in this collection covers three decades of American dinnerware—1930s through 1950s—used with up-to-date verve. I find the colorful glazes pleasing backgrounds for cheeses.

Although it has many imitators scattered throughout the world, Parmigiano Reggiano is the undisputed king of hard cheeses.

GUIDELINES

Cheese in America today is vastly different from what it was even a mere decade ago. To meet the demands of a nation of new connoisseurs, previously unheard of cheeses or those encountered only in European travels are jetted daily to importers across the country. Some European cheese makers have opened branches in the United States to manufacture their products closer to the market. American cheese makers are branching out in new directions to duplicate the classics of other countries now that consumer tastes are more demanding. The array and variety of cheeses in the refrigerated cases of our delicatessens, cheese stores, gourmet groceries, and supermarkets can make selection a bewildering experience.

A few simple guidelines can demystify the experience of buying, storing, and using cheese.

Cheese, according to my desktop Webster, is "a food made from the curds of milk pressed together to form a solid." Like the fermentation of grape juice into wine, cheese making is often shrouded in mystery. In truth, the making of cheese is a simple process that involves some sort of milk, a rennet to curdle the milk for separating the curds from the whey, the introduction of bacteria to set up the ripening process, and a variety of atmospheric conditions to cure the cheese.

Through the centuries, cheese has been made from the milk of any milk-producing animal, from the ass to the zebra. Today it is most commonly made from the milk of cows, goats, or sheep, with a small fraction from water buffaloes. The milk is heated to a point somewhere between 70° F and 100° F, depending on the type of cheese being made. Heating creates a proper environment for lactic-acid organisms to begin work. Next, the same beneficial *Streptococcus* bacteria found in buttermilk or yogurt are introduced into the warm milk to act as a starter and increase the acidity level.

Rennet, an enzyme extracted from the stomach lining of calves or other young animals, or a chemically made rennet substitute is then introduced into the milk, causing curdling, or coagulation, that separates the curds from the whey. The whey, or water, is then drained away and the collected curds are cut, pressed into molds, and exposed to bacteria that set up the ripening process. Natural or controlled atmospheric conditions and other curing techniques such as salting and washing of the rind guide the cheese toward the intended result.

The differences in cheeses come from the way the curds are drained, cut, flavored, and pressed, the bacteria involved, the type and length of curing in caves, cellars, or under refrigeration, the use of saltwater or wine baths, and a host of other subtle to severe variations.

TYPES OF CHEESE

Generally, cheese is grouped into four categories:

Soft. These include the fresh, unripened cheeses such as Cottage, Cream, Farmer, or Pot cheese that need only a starter, perhaps buttermilk, and a few hours before they're ready to eat. More complex soft cheeses include quickly ripened Brie and Camembert, as well as those made with added cream, known as double-crèmes and triple-crèmes; all have thin, white edible rinds with creamy to runny interiors and are ready to eat within a few days or weeks.

Semisoft. Within this group are cheeses ripened three ways: bacteria- or yeast-ripened mildly flavored cheeses such as Italian Fontina and Danish Havarti; assertively flavored American Liederkranz, German Schloss, and others that require surface microorganisms during ripening; and blue-veined cheeses such as Italian Gorgonzola, French Roquefort, and English Stilton that are ripened by the presence of *Penicillium* molds.

Firm. Originally termed "farmhouse" but now mostly made in factories, these cheeses are formed into wheels or blocks, usually with wax coatings to seal out molds and external bacteria. This category includes Cheddar and similar British and American cheeses; Edam, Gouda, and other products from the Netherlands; Caciocavallo, Provolone, and similar Italian cheeses; and cheeses with holes, such as Switzerland's Emmentaler and the "Swiss" types like Norwegian Jarlsberg. These are generally aged a few weeks to more than a year.

Hard. Finally, there are the carefully aged cheeses with grainy textures, that are primarily intended for grating. These include Asiago, Parmesan, and Romano. The aging process takes from one year to over seven years.

The following is a brief shopping list or directory of my own favorite cheeses. Included are some of the world's greatest cheeses that are readily available and a few international treats not easily located. All of the cheeses used in the recipe chapters are listed here.

Soft, Fresh

Chèvre (France, Italy, USA). Goat's milk, mild to pungent, made under a variety of names—Banon, Bucheron, Caprella, Chevresse, Crottin, Montrachet, Pyramide, Saint-Christophe, Taupinière, and so on—and in a variety of shapes, including rounds, cylinders, logs, and pyramids. Many are sold fresh, others are aged or marinated in oil. Some have herbs or peppers added. Officially the term Chèvre indicates French-made goat's milk cheeses, but it has come to be applied to all such cheeses, including very good ones made on the East Coast and in California.

Cream cheese (USA). Cow's milk, soft and slightly tangy, preferably free of the stabilizing gums that are added to the familiar silver-packaged type to increase shelf life.

Feta (Bulgaria, Denmark, Greece). Sheep's milk, preserved in brine, crumbly, salty, slightly sour.

Mascarpone (Italy). Cow's milk, heavy whipped-cream texture, sweet with a hint of acidity.

Mozzarella (Italy, USA). Not the semisoft rubbery stuff in supermarket packages, but freshly made of cow's milk by local cheese makers; the buffalo's milk variety from Italy is highly perishable and thus must be extremely fresh.

Petite-Suisse (France). Cow's milk; extra cream makes it a bit sweeter than domestic Cream cheese.

Ricotta (Italy, USA). Cow's or sheep's milk whey, sometimes with milk added, or buttermilk, bland and creamy; the freshly made product is quite different from the common heavy supermarket type.

Torta (Italy). Layers of various soft cheeses lined with fresh herbs, smoked salmon, figs, or other ingredients. Very rich and festive. A particular favorite, made by Peck's in Milano, layers Mascarpone, soft-ripened Robiola, basil, and pine nuts.

Soft-ripened, Edible Rind

Brie (France, USA). Cow's milk, mild to tangy, high butterfat; be sure it is not overripe, and therefore bitter. Look for superb raw milk versions that occasionally appear.

Boursalt (France). Cow's milk, triple-crème, slightly tangy.

Boursin (France). Cow's milk, very smooth triple-crème, plain or with herbs or peppercorns.

Camembert (France, USA). Cow's milk, mild to tangy, spreadable; avoid overripeness by selecting a cheese with a lightly fruity fragrance.

Explorateur (France). Cow's milk, exceptionally smooth, mild-flavored triple-crème; one of the most exquisite cheeses.

Saint-André (France). Cow's milk, mild, rich and buttery triple-crème.

Vacherin (France, Switzerland). Cow's milk, very creamy and mild. One Vacherin Fribourgeois—Vacherin à Fondue—is used mainly for fondue; another Vacherin Fribourgeois—à la Main—is softer and best as a dessert cheese. Vacherin Mont d'Or, made only during the final months of the year, is creamy and liquid enough to eat with a spoon.

Semisoft, Mild

Bel Paese (Italy). Cow's milk, slightly sweet and buttery. Look for wrapper with map of Italy to distinguish the genuine cheese from the American imitation, on whose wrapper appears a map of the Western Hemisphere.

Fontal (France, Italy). Cow's milk, smooth, similar to Fontina, and in fact was called Fontina until 1951, when the Italian government formally reserved the use of that name for cheese produced in the Val d'Aosta.

Fontina (Italy). Cow's milk, delicately sweet and buttery. One of the true greats! By law, must come from Val d'Aosta, which sits high in the mountains near the borders of France and Switzerland. Pale yellow rind distinguishes it from red-skinned Danish and Swedish imitators; although good, they're not at all like the original. Fontinella is a third-rate American copy.

Havarti (Denmark). Cow's milk, mild yet tangy, creamy with small irregular holes; also known as Danish Tilsit. Some varieties have caraway seeds or other flavorings.

Morbier (France). Cow's milk, buttery with a piquant aftertaste; a layer of edible ash horizontally divides two halves, which were traditionally made from two batches of milk, one from the morning milking and one from the afternoon milking.

Pont l'Evêque (France). Cow's milk, mild to strong, square shape with reed-basket markings.

Port-du-Salut (France). Cow's milk, creamy with a full flavor marked by a bit of tang.

Saint-Nectaire (France). Cow's milk, smooth, slightly nutty.

Taleggio (Italy). Cow's milk, creamy and rich, but a bit tart; square, flat shape.

Semisoft, Assertive, Surface-ripened

Liederkranz (USA). Cow's milk, strong aroma, creamy, surprisingly mellow taste.

Limburger (Belgium, West Germany). Cow's milk, extremely aromatic, creamy, strong. Not for everyone.

Munster (France, West Germany). Cow's milk, very aromatic, tangy. An ancient cheese from the Alsace that is now also produced in West Germany, where it is written with an umlaut— Münster. Both European varieties are quite different from the nondescript American cheese of the same name.

Schloss (Austria, West Germany, USA). Cow's milk, mild version of Limburger.

Semisoft, Blue-veined

Blue Castello (Denmark). Cow's milk, triple-crème, fairly mild.

Bleu de Bresse (France). Cow's milk, creamy. The same company makes Bresse Blue in Wisconsin.

Danablů (Denmark). Cow's milk, very buttery, originally made as a substitute for Roquefort. While good, it isn't a match for the French original.

Gorgonzola (Italy). Cow's milk, soft and creamy yet crumbly. My favorite blue. There is also a rare pure white version.

Maytag Blue (USA). Cow's milk, creamy; made in Iowa.

Roquefort (France). Sheep's milk, strong and crumbly. The real thing, which appears under about a dozen brand names, is highly protected by the French government; each cheese is wrapped in foil and marked with a label on which appears a sheep printed in red.

Stilton (England). Cow's milk, intensely flavored, moist, creamy yet crumbly. Look for tall, cylindrical shape.

Firm, Smooth Cheddar Types

Caerphilly (Wales). Cow's milk, white, buttermilk flavor, slightly salty.

Cantal (France). Cow's milk, slighty sweet and nutty; interior blue veins sometimes appear. Probably the oldest French cheese.

Cheddar (Canada, England, USA, and others). Cow's milk, or some goat's milk, mild to very sharp, naturally cream colored, often dyed orange with annatto. Importation of English Cheddar to the United States is restricted to protect American-made products. My favorites are from Canada, Vermont, upstate New York, and Oregon.

Cheshire (England). Cow's milk, mellow, crumbly. Dyed orange for exportation to suit assumed American preference. England's oldest cheese.

Colby (USA and others). Cow's milk, moister and softer than Cheddar.

Double Gloucester (England). Cow's milk, mellow, usually a creamy golden color; white variety is rare.

Edam (the Netherlands). Cow's milk, smooth, rather bland.

Gjetost (Norway). Goat's milk (or goat and cow's milk), sweet, caramel color and consistency. A little goes a long way.

Gouda (the Netherlands). Cow's milk, supple texture; young Goudas are mild, aged (one year) ones are fuller flavored and tangier.

Kasseri (Greece). Sheep's milk, mild, slightly salty, similar to Italian Provolone. American imitation is made of cow's milk.

Monterey Jack (USA). Cow's milk, mild and sweet, softer than Cheddar. Hard Monterey Jack is made from skimmed or partly skimmed milk and aged six months or longer.

Provolone (Italy and others). Buffalo's or cow's milk, creamy, buttery to piquant, sometimes smoked; may be formed into fanciful shapes.

Wensleydale (England). Cow's milk, smooth, soft, mild yet tangy.

Firm, Swiss Types with Holes

Appenzeller (Switzerland). Cow's milk, smooth and dense, mild to sharp.

Beaufort (France). Cow's milk, slightly salty, very rich French version of Swiss Gruyère.

Emmentaler (Switzerland). Cow's milk, nutty or fruity. This is the real "Swiss" cheese that everyone attempts to copy; I rank it with the best in the world.

Gruyère (Switzerland). Cow's milk, mild to sharp, nutty aroma, creamy but very firm.

Jarlsberg (Norway). Cow's milk, mild to nutty. One of my favorites.

Raclette (Switzerland). Cow's milk, smooth, similar to Gruyère, melts easily.

"Swiss" (USA and many others). Cow's milk; these imitations of Emmentaler run the gamut from very bland to very good, but still not as good as the original.

Hard, Grating

Asiago (Italy, Argentina, USA). Cow's milk, sharper and saltier than Parmesan. Italian version is the best.

Kefalotyri (Greece). Sheep's or goat's milk, similar to Italian grating cheeses.

Parmesan (Italy, Argentina, USA). Cow's milk, sweet to sharp. Only Parmigiano Reggiano, from the area of Emilia-Romagna between Parma and Reggio, may officially be called Italian Parmesan; other similar Italian cheeses must be labeled Grana. Similar cheeses produced outside of Italy are often called Parmesan, but bear little resemblance to the real thing.

Pecorino Romano (Italy). Sheep's milk (or goat and cow's milk), tangy and pungent.

Sapsago (Switzerland). Cow's milk, tangy and spicy, and pale green from the addition of sweet clover.

Sardo (Italy, Argentina). Sheep's milk, tangy. Traditionally made in Sardinia of pure sheep's milk, where it is called Pecorino Sardo; today it is often made with part cow's milk.

PROCESSED CHEESES

Processed cheeses start out as natural cheeses, then are melted to halt their ripening, pasteurized for uniform flavor, and blended with emulsifiers for smooth texture and long shelf life. Many are artificially colored and/or flavored. They melt easily and smoothly; there's no rind, and therefore no waste. Nutritionally, they're about the same as natural cheeses, but lack the aromas, flavors, textures, and character of the great cheeses. Someone gave them the appropriate label "TV dinners of the cheese world."

The French make a few processed cheeses that some people favor: Gourmandise, flavored with kirsch or walnuts; La Grappe, covered with grape seeds; Rembol, masked with crushed peppercorns or walnuts; and Reybier, covered with pistachios or walnuts.

Cheese "foods" are products that contain some real cheese and are found in jars or boxes on the grocery shelves. They have little in common with great cheeses.

CHEESES FOR SPECIAL DIETS

Admittedly, cheese is high in butterfat, and thus highly caloric. Cheeses that are naturally lower in fat and also taste good include low-fat or uncreamed Cottage, Farmer, or Pot cheese, and Ricotta or Mozzarella made with partly skimmed milk. Aimed at our lighter way of eating, manufacturers now offer Cheddar and other cheeses made from nonfat dry milk or partly skimmed milk to reduce the fat content. Most have little flavor. Beware of many "imitation" cheeses that are supposedly lower in fat due to reduced dairy fats; labels may reveal the presence of high levels of saturated palm or coconut oil.

The best diet for optimal health includes all foods, but in moderation. If you're cutting down on the fats, why not occasionally enjoy smaller portions of good cheese. Parmesan and other hard grating cheeses are usually eaten in less quantity, so they add less fat.

If you need to eliminate salt, try American-made salt-free Cheddar or salt-free Gouda from the Netherlands. Both are fairly tasty.

BUYING CHEESE

The most important guideline I can offer any cheese consumer is to buy from a reputable store, preferably one that has frequent turnover to assure freshness. Ask questions and ask for suggestions. Most cheese sellers are happy to share their knowledge, opinions, and preferences. Ask for a taste. Quality stores will always let you taste before making a purchase, unless you're buying prewrapped pieces of cut cheese or prepackaged cheeses such as Camembert.

When buying packaged cheese, check the "pull date," the stamped date that indicates the final day for sale. Good stores will not have expired dated cheeses in their coolers. I prefer the texture and flavor of packaged soft-ripened cheeses about two days before the marked expiration. Even when you go by the dates or the word of the sales personnel, a cheese can be past its prime when the package is opened. Bad cheeses should be returned to the store immediately. A reliable dealer always makes good on cheese that's over the hill when the consumer is not at fault.

When shopping in a good cheese market, I've too often yielded to the temptation to buy a little of this and some of that, ending up with more cheese than I can use within a few days. Since the shelf life of any cut cheese is relatively brief, it's best to buy cheese in small quantity, only what can be used within a day or two for soft cheeses or a couple of weeks for firm or hard types.

STORING

At one time, the most common way to store cheese was to wrap it in cloths that had first been moistened with vinegar and then wrung dry. While a few people still follow this practice, the convenient and ideal way to store cheese is to wrap each piece as tightly as possible in foil or, preferably, see-through plastic wrap, then place the pieces in sealed plastic bags or covered containers in the warmest part of the refrigerator. Such airtight protection is especially important when storing strongly aromatic cheeses.

Glass cheesekeepers have built-in supports to hold well-wrapped cheese over a solution of vinegar and water; the standard ratio is one-fourth teaspoon vinegar to one cup water. If you use this method, change the solution daily, or at least every few days.

For optimum shelf life, rewrap the remaining cheese in fresh foil or plastic wrap each time you cut a piece.

Fresh cheeses, such as Ricotta, Farmer, or Cottage, should be stored in airtight containers and used as quickly as possible. Mozzarella tastes best the day it is made. If you purchase locally made or imported Mozzarella that has been kept in a holding bath, and then must keep it for a day or two longer, submerge it in a solution of water and a bit of skimmed milk. Cover the container and store in the refrigerator; change the liquid daily.

If for some reason you end up with a whole wheel or large chunk of cheese that needs to be stored for a long period, completely cover all surfaces with melted paraffin wax. Wrap tightly in foil and store in the refrigerator.

I often grate bits and pieces of cheese left on the cheese board and refrigerate the grated cheese in airtight containers to have on hand for adding to sauces, soups, casseroles, salads, or pasta. Grated cheese stores well in the refrigerator for about a week. If there's a need to keep it longer, it should be frozen.

No matter how well it is stored, cheese will eventually develop mold. On semisoft, firm, or hard cheeses, mold is part of the natural aging process. Simply cut away and discard the mold and use the good cheese underneath. Soft cheeses that grow mold should be discarded.

A few cheese people report that freezing causes very little if any harm to cheese; most violently oppose the practice. My experiments lead me to believe that hard or Cheddar types can be frozen satisfactorily for up to six months, although there'll be some changes in texture and flavor. Creamy cheeses, including blues, can be frozen for about the same length of time; they will be too crumbly for eating, but are fine for cooking.

If you overbuy and must freeze, be sure the cheese is in good condition. Wrap it airtight in heavy foil or several layers of plastic wrap to preserve as much moisture and flavor as possible. Thaw the cheese slowly in the refrigerator for twenty-four to forty-eight hours before using.

CUTTING

Whether cutting cheese for storing or serving, there is an appropriate cut for each type of cheese. Rounds such as Brie should be cut into wedges like a pie. Cheddar and other wheels are first cut into wedges, then cut again across the point into smaller pieces. Brick shapes are cut across the rectangle. Square cheeses like Pont l'Evêque are usually cut parallel to one side. Logs such as Bucheron are traditionally sliced across the log to make rounds. Pyramid and other wedge shapes are best divided into quarters. Parmesan and similar hard grating cheeses should not be cut; pieces should be pried loose in chunks that follow the natural grain.

When cutting through rinds of colored wax, first make a cut just deep enough to go through the rind, cutting all the way around the rind where the final cut will be. Then wash the knife and cut through the interior. This method avoids bleeding the color and wax from the rind into the cheese.

Cookware stores and cheese markets usually offer a variety of implements for cutting cheeses. Cheese-board knives range from tiny spreaders for soft cheeses, through serrated blades for semisoft cheeses, to miniature hatchets for firm types. When serving an assortment of cheeses, provide a different knife for each cheese to avoid mixing of flavors.

Paddle-shaped cheese slicers, with a blade inside a central opening, permit thin slices of semisoft or firm cheeses. A sharp knife is necessary to form thicker slices. Dipping the knife in warm water between cuts makes slicing some soft and gooey cheeses easier.

If you have need to cut up whole wheels, buy a double-handled knife.

GRATING

Soft cheeses should be grated with a coarse grater, semisoft or firm types with a medium grater, and very dry ones with a medium-fine grater. There are numerous graters on the market and choice is a matter of individual preference.

When it comes to grating, the food processor saves time—and fingers. Firm cheeses can be grated with one of the insert grating blades, while hard cheeses, such as Parmesan, can be first chopped and then "grated" with the steel knife. Just break or cut the cheese into small pieces and put it in the processor bowl. Use the off/on pulse method to begin breaking it up and then let the blade run until the cheese is as fine as you like.

CHEESE COMBINATIONS

Cheese boards, platters, tastings, or other presentations are put together in two ways: an assortment of contrasting cheeses or an array of selections from one group or family.

The contrasts can be in texture, color, richness, or taste, or a combination of these elements. For example, you can set off a fresh cheese that's smooth and white against a mellow well-aged yellow cheese and an assertive blue-veined type. Or do the obvious and contrast a buttery, rich triple-crème with a young goat's milk cheese. Be inventive!

When the presentation includes cheeses from only one group, nibblers can compare the subtleties among national traditions or individual cheese makers. Consider offering blues from England, Italy, and France alongside an American version. Or serve only California-made goat's milk cheeses.

No matter which type of combination you choose, cheese presentations can be the easiest, showiest, and most delicious way to get a party going or end a wonderful meal. They also prompt people to exchange thoughts on what's being tasted, making a cheese selection a great icebreaker. Be sure to include good quality, very fresh bread or crackers, crisp ripe fruits, just-shelled nuts, or other accompaniments that help show off each cheese to its best advantage.

STARTERS

There is nothing better to whet the appetite, accompany drinks, or spark convivial entertaining than the taste of a perfect cheese. For those times when you want a bit more variety, however, the following recipes can be offered as appetizers, snacks, or light first courses. With a few simple additions such as salad or dessert, several of them can be expanded into complete brunch, lunch, or supper dishes.

Spicy Cheese Sticks

1-1/2 cups sifted unbleached all-purpose flour
1 tablespoon baking powder
3/4 teaspoon salt (optional)
1/8 teaspoon cayenne pepper, or to taste
1/3 cup vegetable shortening, chilled
1 cup (about 3 ounces) shredded Cheddar cheese
3 tablespoons minced or grated onion
1 tablespoon Worcestershire sauce
3 or 4 dashes Tabasco sauce, or to taste
2/3 cup buttermilk
2 tablespoons butter, melted
1/4 cup (about 1 ounce) freshly grated Parmesan cheese

Sift together the flour, baking powder, salt, and cayenne pepper into a mixing bowl. Add shortening and cut in with a pastry blender until well incorporated. Stir in Cheddar cheese, onion, and Worcestershire and Tabasco sauces. Add buttermilk and stir to make a soft dough. Wrap in waxed paper or plastic wrap and chill for 1 hour.

Preheat the oven to 475° F.

On a lightly floured board, roll out dough into an 8- x 12-inch rectangle. Wrap loosely around rolling pin and transfer to a cold lightly greased baking sheet. With a metal spatula, cut dough in half lengthwise, then cut across at 1-inch intervals to form the sticks. Brush sticks with melted butter, sprinkle with Parmesan, and bake until lightly browned, about 10 minutes. Immediately remove from baking sheet and serve hot, or cool on wire racks before storing in airtight containers.

Makes 24 sticks.

Gorgonzola Wafers

1/4 pound (1 stick) unsalted butter, at room
    temperature
1/2 pound Gorgonzola or other blue cheese,
    finely crumbled
1 cup unbleached all-purpose flour
3/4 cup pine nuts
1/2 teaspoon salt (optional)

Combine the butter and cheese in a food processor or mixing bowl and blend until creamy. Add flour, pine nuts, and salt. Using palms, form into 2 1-1/2-inch-diameter cylinders, wrap each cylinder in waxed paper or plastic wrap, and refrigerate until well chilled and firm or overnight.

Preheat the oven to 375° F.

Slice chilled dough into rounds about 1/8 inch thick and place about 2 inches apart on cold lightly greased baking sheets. Bake until golden brown, about 12 minutes. Immediately remove from baking sheets and cool on wire racks. Store in airtight containers.

Makes about 30 cookies.

Triple-Crème Shortbread

1 cup (about 10 ounces, untrimmed) Saint-André or
    other triple-crème cheese, at room temperature
    and trimmed of rind
1/4 pound (1 stick) unsalted butter, at room
    temperature
1 teaspoon minced or pressed garlic (optional)
2 cups unbleached all-purpose flour

Combine the cheese, butter, and garlic in a blender or food processor and blend until creamy. Add flour and blend until well mixed. Using palms, form dough into two 2-inch-diameter cylinders, wrap cylinders separately in waxed paper or plastic wrap, and refrigerate until well chilled.

Preheat the oven to 350° F.

Slice chilled dough into rounds about 1/2 inch thick and place rounds about 2 inches apart on cold lightly greased baking sheets. Prick each cookie 2 or 3 times with a fork. Bake cookies until they just begin to turn golden around the edges, about 15 to 20 minutes; tops should not brown. Immediately remove from baking sheets and cool on wire racks. Store in airtight container.

Makes about 30 cookies.

Croques-Messieurs

Vary this French classic by using any good melting cheese and cooked chicken or turkey. Serve whole sandwiches for a light meal or snack.

12 slices whole-wheat or firm-textured white bread
1/4 pound (1 stick) unsalted butter, melted
Dijon-style mustard
3/4 pound Emmentaler or other good melting cheese, thinly sliced or grated
6 thin slices (about 5 ounces) flavorful ham
Clarified butter (see note)

Trim crusts from the bread slices and lightly brush one side of each slice with melted butter. Spread mustard to taste on top of the butter on half of the bread slices. Place a ham slice on top of the mustard, top with cheese, and cover with a slice of bread, buttered side down.

In a large heavy-bottomed skillet or griddle, heat several tablespoons of clarified butter to sizzling. Add sandwiches, reduce the heat to low, and cook, turning once, until golden brown on each side, about 3 to 4 minutes per side. Press down with a spatula or weight down with a skillet while cooking. If necessary, add a bit more butter to the pan when turning. Quickly slice each sandwich into 4 squares or triangles and serve hot.

Serves 6 as a light main dish or snack, or 10 to 12 as appetizers.

NOTE: To clarify butter, melt at least 1/2 pound (2 sticks) butter in a small saucepan over low heat. Remove from the heat and let cool for a few minutes while milk solids settle to the bottom of the pan. Skim the butterfat from the top and strain clear clarified butter into a container; discard milk solids. Keeps indefinitely in the refrigerator.

Cheese Pastry Tarts
with Spicy Shrimp

Family friend Christine Conn, who lives in Jonesville, Louisiana, shared two recipes with me that are teamed up here. The pastry shells can be made ahead of time and frozen in airtight containers until the day you plan to serve the tarts.

CHEESE PASTRY

2 cups unbleached all-purpose flour
1/4 teaspoon cayenne pepper, or to taste
1 teaspoon salt (optional)
1/2 pound (2 sticks) unsalted butter, chilled
2-2/3 cups (about 1/2 pound) grated sharp
  Cheddar cheese

SPICY SHRIMP

8 ounces Cream cheese, at room temperature
2 tablespoons mayonnaise
1 tablespoon Worcestershire sauce
4 to 6 dashes Tabasco sauce
Chili powder
Cayenne pepper
About 3/4 cup pickled cocktail onions
About 1 cup cooked tiny bay shrimp

Herb sprigs or tiny salad greens for garnish

To make the pastry, combine the flour, cayenne pepper, and salt in a mixing bowl. With a pastry blender, cut in butter and cheese until well incorporated and mixture forms a smooth dough. Gather dough into a ball, wrap it in waxed paper or plastic wrap, and chill for several hours or overnight.

To make the filling, combine the Cream cheese, mayonnaise, and Worcestershire sauce in a blender or food processor and blend until smooth. Add Tabasco sauce, chili powder, and cayenne pepper to taste. Add 1/4 cup pickled onions and 1/2 cup shrimp and blend quickly just to chop and incorporate; reserve remaining onions and shrimp for garnish. Filling can be covered and refrigerated for up to 24 hours.

Preheat the oven to 350° F.

Pinch off small portions of the dough and, with fingertips, press onto the bottom and sides of cold lightly greased 3-inch tart pans, 1-1/2-inch tartlet pans, or tiny muffin-tin wells. To prevent pastry from puffing up or shrinking during cooking, line pastry with foil and fill with rice, dried beans, or metal pie weights, or hold in place by nesting ungreased tart pans or muffin tins on top of pastry. Bake until golden brown, about 10 to 15 minutes. Cheese burns easily; be careful not to overcook. Remove weights and cool pastry shells slightly. Invert pans to remove shells. Cool shells completely on wire racks before using or before storing in airtight containers in the freezer for up to 2 months. If frozen, thaw completely in refrigerator before using.

Just before serving, fill pastry shells with cheese mixture and top each with a cocktail onion and a shrimp. Garnish with herb sprigs or greens. Arrange on serving trays.

Makes about 12 3-inch tarts, or 24 bite-sized tartlets.

Hot Crab Mornay

3 to 4 green onions, including tops, finely chopped
1/4 cup minced fresh parsley
4 tablespoons (1/2 stick) butter
1 tablespoon unbleached all-purpose flour
1 cup light cream (half and half)
1 cup (about 3 ounces) shredded Gruyère or other
    Swiss-style cheese
2 teaspoons dry sherry
Salt (optional)
Cayenne pepper
1/2 pound crab meat, flaked

In a medium-sized saucepan over medium heat, sauté onions and parsley in butter until onions are tender. Sprinkle in flour and stir until bubbly, about 2 to 3 minutes. Stirring constantly, slowly add light cream and continue to stir until mixture is smooth. Add cheese, sherry, and salt and cayenne pepper to taste, stirring until cheese melts. Mix in crab meat and simmer until heated through. Transfer to a heat-resistant container over a table burner or votive candle and serve warm with small toasts or raw vegetables.

Makes 3 to 4 cups.

Tomato-Garlic Spread

2 to 3 garlic cloves
3 to 4 whole sun-dried tomatoes in olive oil
1/2 pound creamy Chèvre or regular Cream cheese,
    at room temperature
Oil from sun-dried tomatoes

Place the garlic and tomatoes to taste in a blender or food processor and chop. Add cheese and a little of the olive oil from the sun-dried tomatoes and blend until smooth.

Makes about 1-1/2 cups.

Pimiento-Cheese Spread

3 medium-sized fresh red pimientos or other
    red sweet peppers
2 cups (about 6 ounces) grated high-quality Cheddar
    or similar cheese
2 garlic cloves, minced or pressed
1/4 cup mayonnaise, or to taste
Salt (optional)
Cayenne pepper
Crisp toast, cut into small shapes (optional)
Italian flat-leaf parsley for garnish (optional)

Place the peppers over an open flame or under a broiler and turn frequently until charred on all sides. Place the peppers in a loosely closed paper bag until cool, about 15 minutes. Remove the peppers from the bag and rub off blackened skin with your fingertips. Cut peppers in half, remove and discard seeds and veins, chop the flesh, and reserve.

Place the cheese, garlic, mayonnaise, and salt and cayenne pepper to taste in a blender or food processor and blend until mixture is fairly smooth. Add chopped peppers (reserve a small amount for garnish if serving on toast) and blend just to combine. If desired, spread on toasts and garnish with a bit of reserved pepper and a parsley leaflet.

Makes about 3 cups.

Granny's Onion Dip

This favorite goes back to Mary Knecht, my partner's grandmother, who served it often at our Lake Tahoe compound, as we still do.

3/4 pound Cream cheese, at room temperature
3 tablespoons mayonnaise
2 tablespoons heavy cream or light cream
    (half and half)
1 tablespoon Worcestershire sauce
Salt (optional)
Chopped garlic or onion

Combine the Cream cheese, mayonnaise, cream, Worcestershire sauce, and salt and garlic or onion to taste in a blender or food processor and blend until smooth.

Makes about 2 cups.

Chutney-glazed Cheese

Everything is done ahead of time for this fun addition to the appetizer table. Serve with wheatmeal biscuits, crackers, or bite-sized muffins.

2 pounds Cream cheese, at room temperature
1/2 pound (2 sticks) unsalted butter,
    at room temperature
2 to 3 tablespoons hot or mild curry powder, or to taste
Grated zest and juice of 1 orange
1 cup finely chopped Major Grey's chutney
1 cup roasted whole cashews
Thin strips of orange zest for garnish

Dampen 2 18-inch squares of cheesecloth with water, wring dry, and stack them flat, one on top of the other. Now smoothly line a 5-cup straight-sided container, such as a new flower pot, a mixing bowl, a loaf pan, or a mold, with the double-thickness cheesecloth.

Combine the Cream cheese, butter, and orange zest and juice in a food processor or electric mixer and beat until fluffy. Remove about half of the mixture and reserve. Add curry powder to the remaining mixture and blend until thoroughly mixed. Spoon about one-third of the reserved cheese mixture into the lined mold, pressing with fingers or a spatula to compress the mixture and eliminate air pockets. Add about one-third of the curried cheese mixture, pressing in the same manner. Continue alternately layering the cheese mixtures until each is used. Bring excess cheesecloth up over the top to cover cheese completely and chill until the cheese feels firm when gently pressed, about 1-1/2 hours.

Invert the mold onto a serving plate and gently pull off the cheesecloth. If not serving within a couple of hours, wrap tightly with plastic wrap and refrigerate for up to 2 days.

Place the chutney in a small saucepan and melt over low heat. While the chutney is melting, gently press the cashews into the surface of the cheese. Remove the chutney from the heat and cool to room temperature, then spoon it over the cheese to cover completely; use a small spatula to spread it evenly onto the sides. Refrigerate the mold for about 30 minutes to allow the glaze to set. Garnish with orange zest.

Serves 12.

Pastry Puffs with Mornay

Pastry Puffs (recipe follows)

1 small onion, sliced, or 3 to 4 garlic cloves, bruised

2 cups milk

3 tablespoons butter

3 tablespoons unbleached all-purpose flour

2 egg yolks, beaten

1/4 cup Dijon-style mustard

1 cup (about 3 ounces) grated Gruyère or mild Cheddar cheese

1/2 cup (about 2 ounces) freshly grated Parmesan cheese

3 tablespoons heavy cream

Salt (optional)

Freshly ground white pepper

Freshly grated nutmeg

Make the pastry puffs and reserve.

Place the onion or garlic and milk in a saucepan and simmer for about 10 minutes.

In a heavy-bottomed medium-sized saucepan over medium heat, melt the butter, stir in the flour, and cook, stirring constantly, until bubbly, about 3 minutes. Pour the hot milk through a strainer into the saucepan, discarding the onion or garlic, and stir until the mixture is smooth. Reduce the heat to low and cook, stirring constantly, until the sauce is thick, about 10 minutes. In a small bowl, beat about 2 tablespoons of the sauce into the egg yolks, then whisk into the sauce. Add the mustard, cheeses, and heavy cream, and stir until cheeses are melted and the sauce is smooth. Season to taste with salt, pepper, and nutmeg.

Slice off the top third of each puff and reserve. Fill lower part of each puff with sauce and replace top. Serve hot.

Serves 15 to 20 as appetizers, or 6 to 8 as a main course.

PASTRY PUFFS

1 cup water

1/4 pound (1 stick) unsalted butter, cut into small pieces

1/4 teaspoon salt (optional)

1 cup unbleached all-purpose flour

4 eggs

Preheat the oven to 375° F.

In a large saucepan over medium heat, combine the water, butter, and salt and heat until the butter melts. Remove the saucepan from the heat, add the flour all at once, and stir quickly to blend. Return the mixture to the heat and cook, stirring constantly, until water evaporates and the dough forms a thick mass that pulls away from the sides of the pan. Remove from the heat and cool for 4 to 5 minutes. Add eggs, one at a time, beating well after each addition until mixture is very smooth.

For appetizer-sized puffs, drop small mounds of dough, each about 1 tablespoon in size, onto greased baking sheets, spacing them about 2 to 3 inches apart. For lunch- or dinner-sized puffs, use about 2 tablespoons of dough per puff. With dampened fingertips, smooth and shape each dough mound so that it has a gentle rise in the center. Bake until dough is puffed and browned, about 30 minutes. Turn off the oven, remove the puffs, and prick each puff with a small sharp knife. Return the puffs to the oven until dry and quite firm to the touch, about 10 minutes. Fill immediately and serve hot. Or store the puffs in an airtight container for up to 24 hours. Reheat in a 350° F oven before filling, or spoon warm sauce into room-temperature puffs.

Makes 30 appetizer-sized puffs, or 12 to 15 large puffs.

Chèvre, Eggplant, and Red Pepper Tart

Make your own puff pastry from a reliable recipe or check the supermarket freezer for a high-quality brand that contains only flour, butter, salt, and cream or water.

3 red sweet peppers
4 to 6 slender Japanese eggplants, or 2 small
    globe eggplants
About 1/4 cup virgin olive oil
1 tablespoon minced or pressed garlic
Salt (optional)
Freshly ground black pepper
1/2 pound puff pastry, thawed (in the refrigerator)
    if frozen
4 tablespoons (1/2 stick) unsalted butter, melted
4 cups (about 1 pound) soft mild Chèvre cheese,
    finely crumbled
1/2 cup minced fresh parsley, or 1/2 cup fresh
    basil leaves, cut into thin strips

Place the peppers over an open flame or under a broiler and turn frequently until completely charred on all sides. Place the peppers in a loosely closed paper bag until cool, about 15 minutes. Remove the peppers from the bag and rub off blackened skin with your fingertips. Cut peppers in half lengthwise, remove and discard seeds and veins, and slice the flesh into thin strips. Reserve.

Preheat the oven to 375° F.

Cut unpeeled eggplants crosswise into 1/2-inch-thick slices. Arrange slices in single layers in baking pans or dishes lightly greased with olive oil. Sprinkle with garlic and season to taste with salt and pepper. Drizzle with olive oil and bake until the eggplant is lightly browned and tender but still intact, about 20 minutes.

Increase the oven to 400° F.

On a lightly floured surface, roll out the puff pastry into a 12- x 16-inch rectangle about about 1/8 inch thick. Wrap loosely around the rolling pin and transfer to a lightly greased baking sheet. Alternatively, cut the rectangle into 4- x 6-inch rectangles to form 8 individual tarts and transfer each to the baking sheet with a large spatula.

Leaving a 1-inch border uncovered around the entire perimeter of the pastry, brush the pastry with melted butter and cover with crumbled cheese. Top with the baked eggplant slices and then the roasted pepper strips. (If making individual tarts, distribute cheese, eggplant slices, and pepper strips equally among the 8 pastry pieces.) Brush uncovered pastry edges with water, fold edges in half to form a rim, and press together to make an attractive ridge around the pastry.

Bake until pastry is puffed and golden, about 10 to 15 minutes. Sprinkle with parsley or basil, cut large tart into 2-inch squares, and serve immediately.

Makes about 48 appetizers, or 8 first-course servings.

Chèvre-stuffed Triangles

Flaky *phyllo* dough surrounds tangy goat's milk cheese and a bit of intense tomato flavor. Paper-thin *phyllo* is virtually impossible to make at home. In cities with Greek or Middle Eastern markets, you may locate a source for freshly made pastry; many major supermarkets now carry frozen dough.

1 pound (about 20 sheets) *phyllo* dough, thawed
    (in the refrigerator) if frozen
3/4 to 1 pound (3 to 4 sticks) unsalted butter,
    melted and cooled
1-1/2 cups (about 6 ounces) drained and finely
    crumbled Chèvre cheese in olive oil
About 8 sun-dried tomatoes in olive oil, well
    drained and cut into eighths

Place 1 sheet of *phyllo* on a flat work surface. Keep remaining dough covered with a lightly dampened towel to prevent it from drying out. With a wide pastry brush, lightly brush *phyllo* sheet with cooled melted butter to cover completely. Top *phyllo* sheet with a second sheet and lightly brush it with butter. With a sharp knife, cut the *phyllo* stack lengthwise into 6 equal strips.

Place about 1 teaspoon of crumbled cheese about 1 inch in from the end of a strip, top with a piece of tomato, and fold right-hand corner of *phyllo* end over to opposite side to form a triangle and to cover cheese. Lightly brush the top of the triangle with melted butter. Continue folding in a flag fashion, buttering each fold, until you reach the far end of the strip. Repeat with remaining strips you have already cut and then with the remaining *phyllo* sheets. (At this point, the filled triangles can be covered and refrigerated for up to 2 days before baking, or covered and frozen on baking sheets until firm, then transfered to freezer bags or containers for up to 6 months. Thaw in refrigerator before baking.)

Preheat the oven to 400° F.

Place the *phyllo* triangles, seam side down, about 1-1/2 inches apart on buttered baking sheets. Brush tops with melted butter. Bake until golden brown, about 10 minutes, and serve immediately.

Makes 60 triangles; allow 3 or 4 per person.

VARIATIONS: Allowing about 1-1/2 to 2 cups of filling per pound of *phyllo,* fill with a mixture of puréed cooked spinach and crumbled Feta cheese, any herb- or garlic-flavored cheese, shredded Gouda or other cheese with chopped mushrooms or olives, or any favorite cheese, plain or combined with other ingredients. You might even try a dessert triangle filled with peach-, strawberry-, or chocolate-flavored Cream cheese and sprinkled with powdered sugar after baking.

Blue Cheese Blintzes

Most people are familiar with blintzes, the marvelous Jewish dish of crêpes filled with sweetened cheese and usually served with sour cream and preserves. Here's a not-so-sweet rendition to begin a meal, or to become its centerpiece, set off by a salad.

1 cup (about 1/4 pound) finely crumbled **Bleu de Bresse** or other creamy blue cheese
1/2 cup (about 2 ounces) crumbled **Farmer** or **Cottage cheese**
1 egg yolk, well beaten
3 crisp tart green apples or ripe but firm pears
About 1/4 pound (1 stick) butter
Ground cinnamon or freshly grated nutmeg (optional)
1 cup sifted unbleached all-purpose flour
1/4 teaspoon salt (optional)
1 cup water or milk
2 eggs, well beaten
Crème fraîche

To make the filling, combine the cheeses and egg yolk in a small bowl. Mix with a fork or wire whisk until light and fluffy. Reserve.

Peel, core, and thinly slice the apples or pears. Melt 3 tablespoons butter in a small sauté pan or skillet over medium heat and add apples or pears. Sprinkle with cinnamon or nutmeg to taste and sauté fruit until it is soft but still holds its shape. Remove from the heat and set aside in the pan.

To make the crêpes, sift the flour and salt together into a small mixing bowl. Whisk together the water or milk and eggs in a separate bowl and then stir the mixture into the flour to make a thin batter.

Grease a 7-inch skillet or griddle with butter and heat over medium-high heat until it sizzles. Ladle or pour in about 2 tablespoons batter and tilt the pan to coat the bottom evenly with a thin coating of batter. Cook the crêpe, on one side only, until it begins to curl away from the sides of the pan, about 1 to 2 minutes. Slide the crêpe onto a plate and repeat until all the batter is used up, adding butter to the pan as needed and stacking crêpes as they are cooked. You will have 12 crêpes in all.

Place about 2 to 2-1/2 tablespoons of the cheese filling on the center of the uncooked side of each crêpe. Fold in sides to form small square packages. Melt 2 to 3 tablespoons butter in a skillet over medium-high heat, place 3 to 4 blintzes in the pan, seam side down, and sauté, turning once, until golden brown on both sides, about 2 to 3 minutes in all. While browning the blintzes, quickly reheat sautéed fruit. Serve blintzes at once, topped with warm apple or pear slices and a dollop of crème fraîche.

Serves 6.

Tomato and Mozzarella with Basil Vinaigrette

In this new twist on a traditional antipasto idea, the tomatoes remain intact and are stuffed with cheese for individual servings.

2 tablespoons pine nuts
1 tablespoon balsamic or other red-wine vinegar
1/4 teaspoon minced or pressed garlic
Salt (optional)
Freshly ground black pepper
1/4 cup olive oil
2 tablespoons minced fresh basil
4 medium-sized flavorful ripe tomatoes
1 pound fresh Mozzarella cheese, sliced 1/4 inch thick

Place the pine nuts in a small skillet over medium heat and toast, shaking or stirring continuously, until they begin to turn golden, about 4 to 5 minutes. Empty onto a plate to cool.

To make the vinaigrette, combine the vinegar, garlic, and salt and pepper to taste in a small bowl. Whisk in olive oil until well blended, then stir in basil. Reserve.

Slice off stem end of tomatoes so they will stand upright. With a sharp knife, make deep incisions in the rounded end of each tomato at 1/4-inch intervals, cutting to within 1/2 inch of the stem end. Insert cheese slices into tomato openings. Arrange tomatoes on individual plates and drizzle with vinaigrette. Let stand a few minutes at room temperature for flavors to develop. Sprinkle with toasted pine nuts just before serving.

Serves 4.

Potato and Cheese Salad with Chive Dressing

1/2 pound (about 6 thick slices) bacon,
     preferably pepper cured
2 pounds new or russet potatoes, scrubbed
1/2 cup virgin olive oil
1/4 cup white-wine vinegar
2/3 cup chopped chives
Salt (optional)
Freshly ground black pepper
1/2 pound mild semisoft cheese, cut into 1/2-inch dice
Young lettuces or other greens (optional)

In a skillet, cook the bacon until crisp, remove with a slotted utensil, and drain well on paper toweling. Crumble and reserve.

Place the potatoes in a saucepan with cold water to cover. Bring to a boil over medium-high heat and cook until potatoes are tender when pierced but still hold their shape, about 15 to 25 minutes. Drain the potatoes and peel them as soon as you can handle them. Dice into 1/2-inch cubes and place in a large mixing bowl.

In a small bowl, combine the olive oil, vinegar, chives, and salt and pepper to taste and whisk until blended. Pour over warm potatoes and toss gently. Cool to room temperature and then toss in the reserved crumbled bacon and the diced cheese. Serve plain or on a bed of crisp greens.

Serves 8 to 10.

Fontina and Roasted Peppers

2 medium-sized red sweet peppers
2 medium-sized golden sweet peppers
    (if unavailable, use 4 red peppers)
1/4 cup red-wine vinegar or freshly squeezed
    lemon juice
2 to 3 teaspoons minced or pressed garlic
1 tablespoon fresh oregano leaves, or 1 to 2 teaspoons
    dried oregano leaves, crumbled
Salt (optional)
1/2 cup virgin olive oil
1/2 pound Italian Fontina cheese, sliced 1/8 inch thick
About 1 tablespoon small capers, drained
Fresh oregano sprigs for garnish (optional)

Place the peppers over an open flame or under a broiler and turn frequently until completely charred on all sides. Place the peppers in a loosely closed paper bag until cool, about 15 minutes. Remove the peppers from the bag and rub off blackened skin with fingertips. Cut peppers in half vertically, remove and discard seeds and veins, and slice lengthwise into 1/2-inch-wide strips. Place in a ceramic or glass bowl.

In a small bowl, combine the vinegar or lemon juice, garlic, oregano, and salt to taste. Whisk in olive oil until well blended. Pour over peppers and marinate for at least 6 hours, or for up to 2 days.

Cut cheese into 1/2-inch-wide strips that are as long as the pepper strips. Remove pepper strips from marinade, reserve marinade, and arrange strips on individual plates, alternating them with the cheese strips. Drizzle with a bit of the marinade, sprinkle with a few capers, and garnish with oregano sprigs.

Serves 6 to 8.

Fried Cheese

3/4 cup fine dry bread crumbs
1/4 teaspoon dried oregano leaves, crumbled
1 teaspoon minced or pressed garlic
Salt (optional)
1 egg, beaten
2 tablespoons milk
3/4 cup unbleached all-purpose flour
6 ounces firm cheese such as Cheddar, Mozzarella,
    Gruyère, Chèvre, or Monterey Jack cheese,
    cut into 1/2-inch-thick slices
Vegetable oil for frying
Tomato salsa

Combine the bread crumbs, oregano, garlic, and salt to taste in a small bowl. Whisk together egg and milk in a separate bowl, and place flour in a third bowl.

Dip each cheese slice into the flour, then into the egg mixture, and finally into the seasoned bread crumbs to coat generously. Place coated cheese slices in a single layer on a tray and let stand, uncovered, for 10 to 15 minutes to dry. If the cheese is not completely covered with crumbs, repeat the process.

Meanwhile, pour oil to a depth of 2 inches into a heavy-bottomed sauté pan or deep skillet. Place over medium-high heat and heat until oil is hot but not smoking.

Carefully slide crumb-coated cheese into the hot oil and fry, turning once, until golden, about 2 minutes in all. Do not crowd the cheese slices in the pan or they will not cook properly. Drain briefly on paper toweling and serve piping hot with salsa.

Serves 6.

Parmesan Soup

1 quart light cream (half and half)
5 tablespoons unsalted butter
3 tablespoons unbleached all-purpose flour
2 egg yolks, beaten
1 cup (about 4 ounces) freshly grated Parmesan cheese, preferably Parmigano Reggiano
Salt (optional)
Freshly ground white pepper
Basil Pesto for garnish (see index for recipe)
1 thin slice prosciutto, slivered, for garnish

Place the light cream in a saucepan and scald over medium heat. In a heavy-bottomed saucepan over medium-high heat, melt 4 tablespoons butter, add flour and cook, stirring, until bubbly, about 2 to 3 minutes. While whisking continuously with a wire whisk or stirring with a wooden spoon, add hot light cream in a slow, steady stream. Cook, stirring, until the mixture thickens to the texture of heavy cream, about 5 minutes.

Add a little of the hot soup mixture to the egg yolks and whisk to combine. Slowly add yolks to the soup while whisking. Add cheese and the remaining 1 tablespoon of butter. Stir continuously until the cheese melts and the soup is smooth. Season to taste with salt and pepper. Garnish with swirls of pesto and slivers of prosciutto.

Serves 4.

Swiss Cheese and Potato Soup

When imported Emmentaler is not available, use any flavorful Swiss-type cheese, such as Norwegian Jarlsberg.

4 medium-sized potatoes, peeled and diced
4 tablespoons butter
4 leeks, including most of the green tops, chopped
1 cup dry white wine
6 cups homemade flavorful chicken stock or low-sodium canned chicken broth
1-1/2 cups (about 4-1/2 ounces) shredded Emmentaler cheese
Salt (optional)
Freshly ground white pepper
Freshly grated nutmeg
1 tablespoon chopped chives or dill, or sprigs of either herb, for garnish

Place the potatoes in a saucepan with water to cover. Bring to a boil and cook over medium-high heat for 5 minutes; drain and reserve.

Heat the butter in a saucepan over medium-high heat and sauté the leeks until tender but not browned. Add wine and cook for 2 minutes; add reserved potatoes and chicken stock and cook until potatoes are soft. Working in batches, transfer mixture to a blender or food processor and purée until smooth.

Return soup to pot over low to medium heat. Add cheese and stir with a long-handled wooden spoon until cheese melts and is well blended; do not allow to boil. Season to taste with salt, pepper, and nutmeg. Garnish with chives or dill.

Serves 6 to 8.

Creamy Cheshire Soup

I've used Britain's oldest cheese here, but any Cheddar-type cheese may be substituted.

1/4 pound (1 stick) butter
1/2 cup chopped onion
1/2 cup chopped carrot
1/2 cup chopped celery
1/4 cup unbleached all-purpose flour
1/2 teaspoon baking soda
4 cups homemade flavorful chicken stock or
　　　low-sodium canned chicken broth
4 cups milk, at room temperature
5 cups (about 1 pound) shredded Cheshire cheese
Salt (optional)
Freshly ground white pepper
Cayenne pepper
Paprika
Minced fresh parsley for garnish

Melt the butter in a heavy-bottomed saucepan over medium heat, add onion, carrot, and celery, and sauté until vegetables are tender but not browned, about 5 minutes. Stir in flour and cook, stirring, until bubbly, about 2 to 3 minutes. Stir in baking soda. Pour in chicken stock and milk, blend well, and then add cheese. Stir with a long-handled wooden spoon until cheese melts and the mixture is well blended. Season to taste with salt, white pepper, cayenne pepper, and paprika. Sprinkle with parsley just before serving.

Serves 8 to 10.

Grilled Cheese-stuffed Chilies with Avocado Sauce

Warm chilies filled with a smooth mixture of three cheeses can open a meal or be served as a side dish with grilled meats or fish.

6 fresh mild chili peppers
2 medium-sized ripe avocados
2 garlic cloves, minced or pressed
2 tablespoons freshly squeezed lime juice
Salt (optional)
Freshly ground black pepper
1/4 cup (about 1 ounce) crumbled mild Chèvre cheese
3/4 cup (about 2-1/4 ounces) coarsely grated
　　　Jarlsberg cheese
1/2 cup (about 3 ounces) coarsely grated fresh
　　　Mozzarella cheese
Olive oil
Fried tortilla chips

Prepare the coals or preheat the broiler.

Place the peppers over an open flame, under a broiler, or on a grill and turn frequently until completely charred on all sides. Place the peppers in a loosely closed paper bag until cool, about 15 minutes. Remove the peppers from the bag and carefully rub off blackened skin with fingertips. Leaving stems intact, carefully cut a slit down one side of each chili and remove and discard the seeds and veins.

Pit and peel the avocados. Cut them into chunks and place in a blender or food processor with garlic and lime juice and purée until smooth. Season to taste with salt and pepper. Reserve.

Combine the three cheeses in a bowl, mix together with a fork, and then carefully stuff the mixture into the pepper cavities. Rub chilies with olive oil and grill over a medium-hot charcoal fire or under a broiler until the cheese melts, about 6 to 8 minutes.

Spoon reserved avocado sauce onto individual plates and arrange a chili on each. Serve with tortilla chips.

Serves 6.

HEARTY FARE

Dishes made from cheese can star at a meal. Many of these recipes can be main courses or hearty first courses. Some are side dishes or filling snacks that are easily expanded into a whole meal with the addition of a salad or other accompaniment.

Pizza with Four Cheeses

CRUST

1/2 teaspoon sugar
3/4 cup warm water
1 package (1 tablespoon) active dry yeast
2-1/2 to 3 cups unbleached all-purpose flour
1 teaspoon salt (optional)
1/4 cup olive oil
Coarsely ground cornmeal for dusting

TOPPING

1 cup (about 5 ounces) shredded Italian Fontina cheese
1 cup (about 1/4 pound) crumbled Gorgonzola or
    other blue cheese
1 cup (about 6 ounces) shredded fresh
    Mozzarella cheese
1 cup (about 1/4 pound) freshly grated Parmesan
    cheese, preferably Parmigiano Reggiano
Olive oil for drizzling over cheeses
Fresh herbs, minced or whole leaves, for garnish

To make the crust, dissolve sugar in warm water, stir in yeast, and let stand until foamy, about 5 minutes.

In a large bowl, combine 2 cups of the flour with salt. Make a well in the center and pour in the yeast mixture and 3 tablespoons of the olive oil. Stir with a wooden spoon until flour is incorporated. Gradually add as much of the remaining flour as needed for dough to hold together.

Turn the dough out onto a lightly floured surface and knead it gently with your hands until it loses its stickiness, about 5 minutes. Continue kneading until the dough is smooth, elastic, and shiny. Shape into a ball and place in a lightly oiled bowl, turning to coat dough with oil. Cover the bowl with a cloth towel or plastic wrap and set to rise in a warm place until doubled in bulk, about 1 to 1-1/2 hours.

Punch down the risen dough and knead it for about 30 seconds. Reserve one-fourth of the dough and form the rest into a ball. Roll the ball out on a lightly floured surface into a round about 12 inches in diameter and 1/4 inch thick. Fold about 1/2 inch of the entire outer edge of the round under and pinch the edge to the dough round to form a raised rim. Divide the reserved dough in half and, with your palms, roll each half into a rope the length of the diameter of the pizza. Place the ropes perpendicular to each other across the pizza to divide it into even quarters. Press the rope ends securely to the edges of the dough round. Sprinkle a baking sheet with cornmeal and carefully transfer crust to the sheet. Cover with a towel and let rise in a warm place for about 20 minutes while oven preheats.

Line the oven bottom with unglazed quarry tiles or place a specially designed pizza stone on a rack that has been positioned as low as possible in the oven. Preheat the oven to 500° F.

Brush the dough with the remaining 1 tablespoon olive oil. Dust a wide spatula or pizza peel with cornmeal, slip the crust onto it, and then slide crust onto preheated tiles or pizza stone. Bake for 7 to 8 minutes and remove from the oven. Add each of the 4 cheeses to a different section of the crust, drizzle with olive oil, return to the oven, and bake until the crust is well browned and the cheeses are melted, about 7 to 10 minutes. Remove from the oven, sprinkle with fresh herbs if desired, and serve piping hot.

Serves 2 to 4.

Raclette with Rosemary Potatoes

Fireside feasting on melted cheese dates back at least one thousand years, to when shepherds in the Swiss Alps first placed chunks of cheese by their evening fire. The Swiss tradition is called *raclette,* a word taken from the French verb *racler,* "to scrape," which is exactly what you do with the melting cheese. It's then eaten with whatever accompaniments are on hand. Tradition calls for boiled new potatoes, but I find roasting them in garlic and rosemary-flavored olive oil adds an appealing new dimension to the dish.

Several Swiss cheeses were originally used for *raclette.* Now both the Swiss and the French make a firm yet creamy cheese simply called Raclette. When unavailable, Swiss Gruyère is superb, as is Appenzeller, Vacherin, and Emmentaler, although the latter must be carefully watched to prevent it from overcooking and turning rubbery. Virtually any firm or semisoft cheese, no matter what the nationality, can be used, even those with added peppers or herbs.

24 or more tiny new potatoes, scrubbed
1/2 cup virgin olive oil
2 to 3 garlic cloves, chopped
1 to 2 teaspoons fresh or dried rosemary leaves
Salt (optional)
About 1 cup gherkins or cornichons
About 1 cup boiled pearl onions or pickled
    cocktail onions
1 French-style baguette, sliced
1/2 pound flavorful smoked ham, cut into strips
1/4 pound salami, thinly sliced
2 to 3 crisp green apples or buttery ripe pears,
    cored and sliced
Half a wheel or a 2- to 3-pound wedge Raclette cheese
Freshly ground black pepper

Preheat the oven to 375° F.

Place the potatoes in a roasting pan or ovenproof skillet. Add olive oil, garlic, rosemary, and salt to taste and turn potatoes in the seasonings to coat all sides. Roast, stirring occasionally, until the potatoes are tender when pierced, about 35 to 45 minutes. If potatoes are not tiny, cut in half or quarters after roasting.

Arrange potatoes, gherkins or cornichons, onions, bread, ham, salami, and apples in separate containers and preheat a plate for each person.

Place the cheese on a heatproof tray with cut side near a fireplace or other heat source, or in a specially designed *raclette* cooker with a built-in heat source (see note). As the cheese melts, scrape off the melted portion with the back of a knife blade and transfer it to the serving plates. Diners make their own selections from the assortment of accompaniments. Serve with a Swiss white wine or any dry white wine that is light and slightly tart, such as Sauvignon Blanc, Alsace Riesling, or Pouilly Fumé.

Serves 4 to 6 as a main course, or 8 to 12 as appetizers.

NOTE: Several versions of tabletop *raclette* cookers are available in cheese shops and cookware stores. Some have heat sources for melting large chunks of cheese; others have individual pans for melting pieces of cheese under heat coils. When using one with individual pans, precut cheese into thick slices that will fit into the pans and offer the cheese in a basket or stacked on a tray, keeping it covered until time to use. Allow about 10 minutes for heating elements to reach correct temperature before beginning.

Neuchâtel-style Fondue

It's unfortunate that fondue keeps passing in and out of vogue in America. This classic Swiss dish is especially satisfying on a cold winter's night and is a fun and easy way to entertain. If you haven't indulged in fondue in awhile, dig out those old utensils or adapt what you have on hand and enjoy.

Originating with the Wavre family in Switzerland, this recipe made its way to the Aylett Cottons, my California family. A crunchy green salad, chilled white wine, and fruit dessert round out the meal.

8 cups (about 1-1/2 pounds) grated Emmentaler cheese
6 cups (about 1-1/2 pounds) grated Gruyère cheese
2-2/3 cups (about 1/2 pound) grated Monterey Jack cheese
1 to 2 garlic cloves
3 tablespoons unsalted butter
2 cups dry white wine
3 tablespoons cornstarch
Salt (optional)
Freshly ground black pepper
Freshly grated nutmeg
1 cup kirsch liqueur
1 to 2 French-style baguettes, sliced 1/2 inch thick, then slices cut into bite-sized pieces
Additional kirsch liqueur for dipping

Combine the cheeses in a large mixing bowl and reserve.

Cut the garlic cloves in half. Rub the interior of a chafing dish, fondue pot, or any container that evenly distributes heat with the cut surfaces of the cloves. Place the vessel over medium heat and melt the butter in it. Combine the wine and cornstarch, stirring until cornstarch is dissolved, then add to the melted butter. When the wine is hot but not boiling, add a handful of the cheese and stir in one direction with a wooden spoon until the cheese melts and the mixture is quite smooth. Continue adding cheese, a handful at a time, and stirring until it has all melted. Season to taste with salt, pepper, and nutmeg. Stir the kirsch into the cheese to heat just before serving.

Place the pot of melted cheese over a votive candle or very low flame. Put the bread in a basket or other container alongside. Provide long-handled fondue forks or skewers for each person to spear bread for dipping. Offer small containers of kirsch for those who wish to dip bread into the liqueur before dipping it into the fondue.

Serves 8 as a main course, or 12 to 14 as a first course.

NOTE: Leftover fondue can be stored in a plastic container and added to soups or pastas.

Polenta
with Italian Fonduta

As a change of pace from pasta, serve this rich south-of-the-Alps cousin of fondue poured over grilled polenta as a first course for dinner or a main dish for lunch or a late supper.

6 cups water
1 tablespoon salt (optional)
2 cups polenta or coarsely ground yellow cornmeal
1/4 pound (1 stick) butter, cut into pieces
1-1/2 teaspoons cornstarch
1 cup light cream (half and half)
5 cups (about 1-1/2 pounds) coarsely chopped
     Italian Fontina cheese
4 egg yolks
Salt (optional)
Freshly ground white pepper
About 3 tablespoons vegetable oil or butter (optional)
Fresh or preserved black or white truffles, thinly sliced
     (optional)

In a copper polenta pan or tall-sided saucepan, bring the water to boil over high heat. Add salt and reduce heat so the water is at a simmer. While stirring continuously with a long-handled wooden spoon, add the polenta in a slow, steady stream. Cook, stirring quite frequently, until polenta is thick enough for spoon to stand upright, about 15 to 20 minutes. Add butter and stir until melted. Pour polenta onto a wooden board or a round platter, or into a buttered 9- x 5-inch loaf pan. Smooth top with dampened wooden spoon. Cool completely before cutting into wedges or slicing as you would bread.

Dissolve the cornstarch in 3/4 cup light cream. Combine with the cheese in a medium-sized heavy saucepan over low heat. Stirring constantly, cook until cheese melts, about 5 minutes. Do not worry if mixture is not smooth at this point.

Preheat the broiler.

With a wire whisk or a fork, whisk together the egg yolks and the remaining 1/4 cup light cream. Add about 1/4 cup of the cheese mixture to the egg mixture, whisking to blend. While whisking constantly, slowly pour the egg and cheese mixture into the melted cheese. Add salt and pepper to taste. Cook over low heat, stirring constantly, until smooth and creamy.

Meanwhile, broil the polenta slices or wedges until lightly golden. Alternatively, grill the polenta slices over charcoal or pan fry them in a little vegetable oil or butter.

Arrange 2 or 3 polenta slices on individual plates and pour warm cheese sauce over them. Top with as many truffle slices as taste and budget allow.

Serves 8 as a first course, or 6 as a main course.

Pasta with
Four American Cheeses

I've Americanized this Italian classic by using four cheeses made in the United States. If you want to stay old-world, use Fontina, Gorgonzola, Provolone or Bel Paese, and real Parmesan.

1 pound fresh fettuccine or dried pasta such as
    spaghetti or tubular macaroni
1/4 pound (1 stick) unsalted butter
1 cup (about 1/4 pound) crumbled California
    Taupinière or other goat's milk cheese
1 cup (about 1/4 pound) crumbled Maytag Blue cheese
1 cup (about 3 ounces) grated Wisconsin Brick cheese
1/2 cup (about 2 ounces) freshly grated aged
    Monterey Jack or domestic Parmesan cheese
1 cup heavy cream
Salt (optional)
Freshly ground black pepper
Freshly grated nutmeg

Cook the pasta in at least 4 quarts rapidly boiling water until *al dente.* Drain.

Meanwhile, melt the butter in a large heavy-bottomed saucepan over medium-low heat. Add Taupinière, Maytag Blue, and Brick cheeses, and cook, stirring constantly, until cheeses melt and the mixture is smooth. Add Jack or Parmesan and heavy cream and stir until well blended and smooth; do not let the sauce boil. Season to taste with salt, pepper, and nutmeg. Add drained pasta, toss, and serve immediately.

Serves 6, small portions please.

Croissants and Cheese

On those rare occasions when I indulge in a croissant, I like it plain with a little jam. Since many people are hooked on these flaky pastries, however, I am including this easy-to-prepare festive dish that is perfect for brunch or supper.

1/2 pound (about 6 thick slices) bacon
3 to 5 croissants, depending on size
5 or 6 eggs, well beaten
1 cup milk
Salt (optional)
Freshly ground black pepper
2 cups (about 6 ounces) finely grated Gruyère cheese
1/4 pound fresh Mozzarella cheese, thinly sliced
1/2 cup (about 2 ounces) freshly grated
    Parmesan cheese
Freshly grated nutmeg
Minced fresh parsley or chervil for garnish

In a skillet, cook the bacon until crisp, remove with a slotted utensil, and drain well on paper toweling. Crumble and reserve.

Preheat the oven to 350° F.

Split the croissants in half lengthwise and place bottoms, cut side up, in one layer in a well-buttered casserole.

Whisk together the eggs and milk and pour about half the mixture over the croissants. Layer the croissants with most of the Gruyère cheese, then the bacon, and finally the Mozzarella cheese. Cover evenly with the remaining egg mixture. Top with the croissant tops, cut side down, and sprinkle with remaining Gruyère, the Parmesan, and a sprinkling of nutmeg. Bake until cheese is melted, the interior is set, and cheese on top is bubbly, about 35 to 45 minutes. Cover the casserole with foil if the croissants seem to be browning too quickly. Sprinkle with parsley or chervil before serving. Cut with a spoon to serve.

Serves 6 to 8.

Cheese Grits Soufflé

From the Deep South come normally heavy cheese grits lightened into a soufflé that's good as a lunch or supper dish along with a salad. For a heartier meal, serve with roasted or grilled meats and vegetables.

6 tablespoons (3/4 stick) butter
1 tablespoon minced or pressed garlic
3 cups water
1/2 teaspoon salt (optional)
3/4 cup quick-cooking white grits
1-1/2 cups milk
6 tablespoons unbleached all-purpose flour
1 cup (about 3 ounces) Monterey Jack cheese, grated
1/2 cup (about 2 ounces) freshly grated Parmesan
    cheese
4 eggs, separated
Salt (optional)
Freshly ground white pepper

Melt 2 tablespoons butter in a small saucepan over low heat. Add garlic and cook until soft but not brown, about 2 minutes. Remove from the heat and reserve.

Preheat the oven to 350° F.

Bring water to a boil in a large saucepan over high heat. Add salt and slowly stir in grits. Return to a boil, reduce heat to low, and cook, stirring constantly, for 5 minutes. Remove from the heat and stir in reserved garlic butter. Reserve.

Place the milk in a saucepan and scald over medium heat. Melt the remaining 4 tablespoons butter in a small saucepan, add flour, and cook, stirring, until bubbly, about 2 to 3 minutes. Pour in the milk and cook, stirring with a wire whisk or wooden spoon, until smooth and thick, about 4 to 5 minutes. Add cheeses and stir until melted; remove from the heat and let cool. Beat in egg yolks one at a time, then combine the cheese sauce with the reserved garlic grits, adding salt and pepper to taste.

Beat the egg whites with a wire whisk or electric beaters until they form stiff peaks. Stir a couple tablespoons of the whites into the cheese grits and then gently fold in the remaining whites. Pour into a buttered 2-quart soufflé dish. Bake until puffed and golden brown on top but still moist inside, about 20 to 25 minutes. Serve immediately.

Serves 4.

Bacon and Cheese Spoon Bread

Old-fashioned spoon bread is a hearty addition to the brunch, lunch, or dinner table. To make a "white" version, use white cornmeal, cream-colored Cheddar, and white corn kernels.

1/2 pound (about 6 thick slices) bacon
1-3/4 cups water
3/4 cup coarsely ground yellow cornmeal
2 cups (about 6 ounces) grated sharp Cheddar cheese
4 tablespoons (1/2 stick) butter, at room temperature
2 garlic cloves, minced or pressed
1/2 teaspoon salt (optional)
Freshly ground black pepper
1 cup buttermilk
4 eggs, separated
3/4 cup fresh corn kernels (cut from about 4 ears)

In a skillet, cook the bacon until crisp, remove with a slotted utensil, and drain well on paper toweling. Crumble and reserve.

Preheat the oven to 350° F.

Bring the water to a simmer in a medium-sized saucepan over medium heat. Add cornmeal in a slow, steady stream while stirring continuously with a wire whisk. Reduce heat to low, and cook, stirring constantly, until the mixture is smooth and thick, about 3 minutes. Remove from the heat, add cheese, butter, garlic, salt, and pepper to taste, and stir until cheese melts. Gradually pour in the buttermilk, stirring constantly. Lightly beat the egg yolks and stir them in with the corn kernels and most of the bacon, reserving a little for topping.

Beat the egg whites with a wire whisk or electric beater until stiff peaks form. Stir a couple tablespoons of the whites into the cornmeal mixture and then gently fold in the remaining whites. Pour into a buttered 2-quart soufflé dish or casserole. Sprinkle remaining bacon on top and bake until firm and golden brown, about 50 to 55 minutes. Serve bread hot; use a big spoon for scooping out the servings.

Serves 6.

Stacked Cheese Enchiladas with Mole Sauce

Mole sauce is a complex blend of herbs, spices, and other ingredients used extensively in southern Mexico. Make your own from a favorite recipe or, as the recipe directs, use the paste available in jars in major supermarkets or Latin markets. If you prefer, roll the tortillas around the filling instead of layering it between them. Alternatively, add cooked meat or seafood along with the cheese.

1/4 cup sesame seeds
1 cup *mole* paste
3-1/2 cups homemade flavorful chicken stock or
    low-sodium canned chicken broth
Vegetable oil for frying
1 dozen corn tortillas
5 cups (about 1 pound) grated mild Monterey Jack or
    Cheddar cheese
1 red onion, thinly sliced and separated into rings
1/2 cup chopped pitted ripe olives
1/2 cup chopped fresh or canned mild or hot
    chili peppers
Red onion rings for garnish
Whole ripe olives for garnish
Sour cream for garnish
Fresh cilantro (coriander) leaves for garnish
Fresh Tomato Salsa

Put the sesame seeds in a small skillet over medium heat, and toast the seeds, stirring or shaking the pan, until golden, about 5 minutes. Empty onto a plate to cool.

To make the sauce, spoon the *mole* paste into a medium-sized saucepan over medium heat. While slowly adding the chicken stock, stir constantly to form a smooth mixture. Bring to a boil, then reduce the heat to keep the sauce warm while frying the tortillas.

Preheat the oven to 350° F.

Pour oil to a depth of 1/4 inch in a large skillet and heat over medium-high heat. One at a time, fry the tortillas briefly in oil to heat and freshen, then dip them into the warm sauce. Place 1 tortilla in the bottom of a lightly greased ovenproof dish or casserole. Top with a thin layer of cheese, a few onion rings, and a sprinkling each of chopped olives and chilies. Continue this procedure until all the tortillas and other ingredients are used, ending with a layer of cheese.

Cover the dish tightly with foil and cook until cheese is melted, about 15 minutes. Garnish with the toasted sesame seeds, additional onion rings, whole olives, a dollop of sour cream, and cilantro leaves. Serve hot, cutting into wedges at the table. Pass the salsa.

Serves 4 to 6.

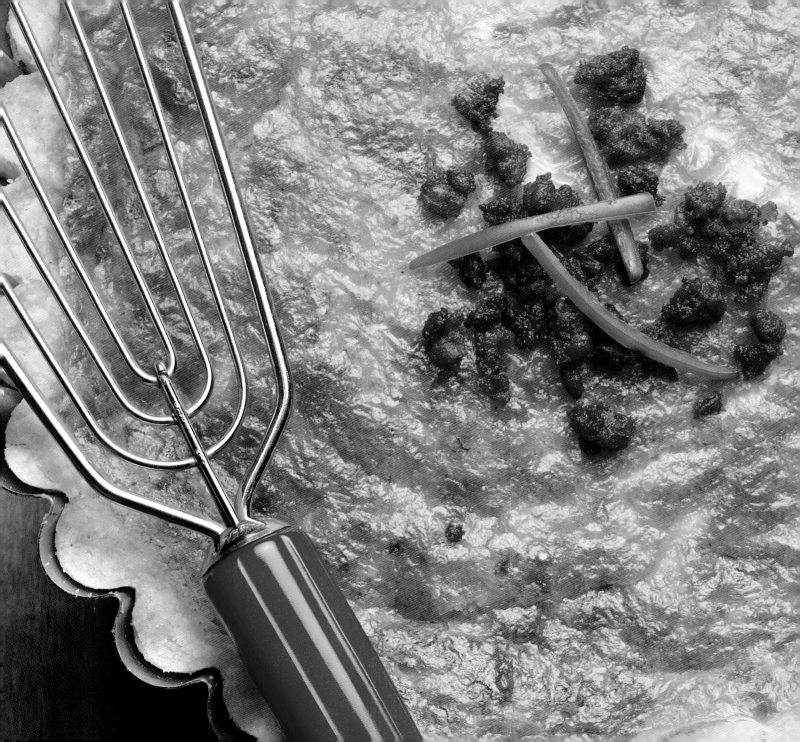

Chili and Chorizo Quiche

The taste buds of even real men should be sparked by this Mexican-inspired variation of the French custard-and-cheese pie.

1 10-inch Paté Brisée crust (recipe follows,
    or use your favorite pastry), unbaked
1/4 pound good-quality chorizo or other spicy
    pork sausage
1/4 cup minced onion
1 tablespoon butter
1 teaspoon minced or pressed garlic
1/4 cup minced fresh green or red hot or mild chili
    peppers, or to taste
3 eggs
2 cups light cream (half and half)
1/4 teaspoon salt (optional)
Pinch cayenne pepper, or to taste
1/2 cup (about 1-1/2 ounces) grated Monterey Jack
    cheese
1/4 cup (about 3/4 ounce) grated Cheddar cheese

Prepare the crust and set aside.

If chorizo is in casing, remove and crumble. In a medium-sized skillet over medium heat, cook chorizo until done; remove from the skillet with a slotted utensil and drain on paper toweling. Reserve.

In a small skillet over medium-high heat, sauté the onion in butter until tender, about 5 minutes. Add garlic and chilies and cook for 2 minutes. Reserve.

Preheat the oven to 375° F.

In a mixing bowl, beat together the eggs, cream, salt, and cayenne pepper. Add cheeses, reserved cooked sausage, and onion mixture and stir to blend. Pour into unbaked pastry shell and bake until the center is set,

about 30 minutes. Let stand 5 to 10 minutes, then cut into wedges. Serve hot or at room temperature.

Serves 6.

PATÉ BRISÉE

1-1/2 cups unbleached all-purpose flour
1/4 teaspoon sugar
6 ounces (1-1/2 sticks) unsalted butter, chilled
    or frozen
2 tablespoons vegetable shortening, chilled
2 tablespoons ice water

Combine the flour and sugar in a mixing bowl. Cut the butter and shortening into small pieces. Add them to the dry ingredients and cut them in with a pastry blender until the mixture resembles coarse cornmeal. Sprinkle with the ice water and mix with a fork just enough to bring the dough together. With your hands, gather the dough into a ball, wrap in a lightly dampened towel or plastic wrap, and refrigerate 1 hour.

On a lightly floured board or pastry cloth, roll out dough into a round about 13 inches in diameter. Wrap loosely around the rolling pin and transfer to a 10-inch quiche dish. Trim edge of round so that only a 1/2-inch overhang remains. Bring pastry overhang inward, folding it so that it is even with the rim of the dish. Press the dough layers together to seal and form an attractive edge.

Makes 1 10-inch quiche crust.

Greek Macaroni with Spicy Meat and Creamy Cheese Sauces

Pastitsio is a baked casserole that combines pasta, a spicy meat sauce, and a creamy cheese sauce. For authenticity use imported Kefalotyri, Greece's hard grating cheese made from the milk of sheep or goats. Serve with a tomato and cucumber salad and perhaps a lemon-flavored dessert.

3/4 pound elbow or interestingly shaped macaroni
6 ounces (1-1/2 sticks) unsalted butter
1 cup finely chopped onion
1-1/2 pounds ground lamb or lean beef
1-1/2 cups puréed canned Italian-style tomatoes
1 teaspoon dried oregano leaves, crumbled
1-1/2 teaspoons ground cinnamon, or to taste
1/2 teaspoon ground cardamom, or to taste
1/4 teaspoon ground cloves, or to taste
1/2 teaspoon ground ginger, or to taste
Salt (optional)
Freshly ground black pepper
1/2 cup unbleached all-purpose flour
2 cups milk
1 cup homemade flavorful chicken stock or
    low-sodium canned chicken broth
1 cup heavy cream
4 egg yolks
1-1/2 cups (about 12 ounces) freshly grated Kefalotyri
    or Parmesan cheese
Freshly grated nutmeg

Cook the macaroni in plenty of boiling water until *al dente.* Drain, toss with 2 tablespoons butter, and set aside.

In a sauté pan or large skillet, melt 2 tablespoons butter over medium heat and sauté the onion until wilted. Add the meat, breaking up lumps with a wooden spoon, and cook just until the pink color disappears. Stir in the tomato purée, oregano, cinnamon, cardamom, cloves, ginger, and salt and pepper to taste. Remove from the heat and reserve.

Preheat the oven to 350° F.

Melt the remaining 1/4 pound butter in a saucepan. Add the flour and cook, stirring, until bubbly, about 2 to 3 minutes. Stirring constantly, slowly add the milk and chicken stock and cook, continuing to stir, until the mixture is thick and smooth, about 8 to 10 minutes. Beat the heavy cream and egg yolks together in a small bowl, add about 2 tablespoons of the hot white sauce, stir to combine, and slowly add the egg mixture to the sauce, stirring with a wooden spoon or wire whisk until smooth. Add 1 cup cheese and stir until melted and smooth; do not allow to boil. Add nutmeg to taste; be generous. Remove from the heat and reserve.

Place half the cooked macaroni in a buttered 3-quart square or rectangular casserole dish or shallow pan. Spoon the meat sauce evenly over the macaroni layer, then top with the remaining macaroni. Cover with the cream sauce and sprinkle with the remaining 1/2 cup cheese and sprinkle with nutmeg. Bake until bubbly, about 35 minutes. Remove from the oven and let stand until lukewarm, about 20 minutes. Slice into squares and serve.

Serves 8.

Melted Cheese Sandwich Pesto

Basil Pesto (recipe follows)
4 slices hearty country-style whole-wheat bread, or
    2 English muffins, split
Unsalted butter or mayonnaise
1 avocado, pitted, peeled, and sliced
8 slices flavorful ripe tomato
1/2 cup (about 3 ounces) grated Monterey Jack or
    Canadian Cheddar cheese

Preheat the broiler.

Spread one side of bread slices or muffin halves with butter or mayonnaise and pesto to taste. Distribute avocado slices over the dressed bread, top with tomato slices, and place under the broiler until tomato is soft. Remove from the broiler, top with cheese and a bit more pesto, and return to the broiler until cheese melts. Serve immediately.

Serves 2 to 4.

BASIL PESTO

2 garlic cloves
2 tablespoons pine nuts
1 cup firmly packed fresh basil leaves
3 tablespoons (about 1 ounce) freshly grated
    Parmesan cheese
3 tablespoons (about 1 ounce) freshly grated
    Pecorino Romano or Pecorino Sardo cheese
1/4 cup virgin olive oil

Place the garlic in a blender or food processor and mince. Add pine nuts and basil and purée until blended but not completely smooth. Add cheese and olive oil and blend briefly.

Makes about 1 cup.

Fried Cheese-filled Pastries

In Florence, while my partner, Lin Cotton, and I were eating our way through Italy for my *Adventures in Italian Cooking,* we noticed dozens of people walking along and eating hot cheese-filled pastries, held in paper cones. Since we both love anything with gooey cheese, we hurried in the direction from which the Florentines were coming, following a trail of discarded wrappers. Our sleuthing paid off in a narrow alley, where we found a hole-in-the-wall that specialized in these little treats known as *panzarotti.*

PASTRY

6 cups unbleached all-purpose flour
1-1/2 teaspoons salt (optional)
6 tablespoons unsalted butter
6 tablespoons vegetable shortening, chilled
3 egg yolks
Milk

FILLING

1-1/2 cups (about 1/2 pound) shredded fresh
    Mozzarella cheese, soaked in 1-1/2 tablespoons
    olive oil
1/2 cup (about 2 ounces) freshly grated Parmesan
    cheese
1/4 pound prosciutto or other flavorful ham, slivered
2 eggs, beaten
1/2 cup seeded, chopped, and well-drained fresh or
    canned Italian-style tomatoes
2 tablespoons chopped fresh parsley
Salt (optional)
Freshly ground black pepper

Vegetable oil for frying

To make the pastry, combine the flour and salt in a mixing bowl and cut in butter and shortening with a pastry blender until the mixture is the consistency of cornmeal. Add egg yolks and mix well. Add a little milk as needed to make a fine, pliable dough. Turn dough out onto a lightly floured surface and knead until smooth and elastic, about 5 minutes. Cover dough with a cloth towel and let rest for 30 minutes.

To make the filling, combine the cheeses, prosciutto or ham, eggs, tomatoes, parsley, and salt and pepper to taste. Mix thoroughly.

Pour vegetable oil into a small saucepan or deep skillet to a depth of about 4 inches. Heat oil to about 365° F, or until a small crust of bread sizzles within seconds of being dropped in the oil.

On a lightly floured surface, roll out pastry 1/8 inch thick and cut into about 12 5-inch rounds. Hold a dough round in the palm of one hand, spoon about 1/4 cup of the filling onto the center of the dough, and moisten edges of round with water. Bring up edges to meet around filling and press them together, sealing tightly to form a round ball. (Or lay the dough round on a flat surface, spoon filling onto one half, bring the other half over the filling to form a half-moon shape, and press together.)

Fry 2 or 3 pastries at a time until golden brown, about 5 to 6 minutes. Remove with a slotted spoon and drain on paper toweling. Serve piping hot, wrapped in a waxed-paper cone if you wish to be authentic.

Serves 6 to 8.

Prosciutto and Chicken Camembert

This easily prepared, elegant main dish is good with buttered noodles.

4 chicken breast halves
4 thin slices prosciutto or other flavorful ham
4 1/4-inch-thick slices Camembert cheese
Salt (optional)
Freshly ground white pepper
2 tablespoons butter, melted
Zest of 1/2 lemon, slivered

Prepare the coals or preheat the broiler.

Skin and bone the chicken breasts, removing tendons and fat. Place each half breast between sheets of waxed paper and pound with a wooden mallet or similar utensil to a uniform thickness of about 1/8 inch. Trim prosciutto and cheese slices to the same dimensions as the chicken breasts; reserve.

Season the chicken to taste with salt and pepper and brush with melted butter. Grill over charcoal or under broiler for 2 minutes. Turn chicken and top each piece with a slice of prosciutto and then a slice of cheese. Grill or broil until cheese melts, about 2 minutes. Sprinkle with lemon zest and serve immediately.

Serves 4.

Gruyère-stuffed Beef Fillet

Pan drippings create a wonderful sauce for this dramatic entrée that's presented whole at the table and then carved.

1 whole beef fillet (about 4 to 5 pounds, excluding
    tail portion; see note)
Salt (optional)
Coarsely cracked black pepper
1/4 cup olive oil
6 thin slices smoked ham
1/2 pound Gruyère cheese, sliced into 12 pieces
12 small shallots or large garlic cloves, unpeeled
8 to 10 fresh or dried whole sage leaves
1 cup full-bodied dry red wine
Fresh whole sage leaves or minced fresh parsley
    for garnish

Preheat the oven to 500° F.

Carefully remove all fat and sinew from the fillet. Season to taste with salt and press a generous amount of pepper into all sides of the meat. Heat olive oil almost to the smoking point in a large heavy-bottomed sauté pan or skillet over high heat. Gently slip the meat into the pan. Brown completely on one side, then turn and brown on all remaining sides. Remove the meat from the pan and let cool slightly. Make 6 deep cuts crosswise at regular intervals along the length of the fillet to create pockets. Place a piece of ham between 2 pieces of cheese and insert the "sandwich" into a pocket of the fillet. Repeat with remaining ham and cheese slices.

Place the stuffed fillet, uncovered, on a rack in a roasting pan. Insert a meat thermometer into the fillet. Surround the meat with the unpeeled shallots or garlic cloves and the sage leaves and pour the wine over them. Place in the oven and immediately turn heat down to 350° F. Roast until the internal temperature of the meat reaches 120° F for rare and the cheese is melted, about 30 minutes.

Remove the fillet from the oven and transfer to a serving platter; cover it with foil to keep it warm. With a slotted spoon, remove the shallots or garlic and scatter them around the meat. Place the roasting pan over high heat and, scraping the pan bottom with a wooden spoon, quickly reduce drippings to about 1 cup of sauce. Pour the sauce into a small pitcher or gravy boat. Remove the foil and garnish the fillet with fresh sage or parsley. At the table, finish slicing through the fillet and serve each piece topped with a layer of melted cheese and ham. Pass the sauce.

Serves 6.

NOTE: If you have to buy the tenderloin with the tail thin portion intact, remove the tail and reserve it for another use.

ENDINGS

Nearly every Italian meal ends with cheese, eaten alone or with fruit. French dining almost always includes a cheese course after the main and salad courses. At last, Americans are discovering the pleasure of topping off a good meal with a bit of cheese, or the endless delicious combinations of cheeses and fruits that can precede or take the place of dessert.

Meal's end cheeses can be just about anything you wish, but blues, double- or triple-crèmes, flavored creams, thin-rind creamy Bries, and fresh young cheeses seem most appropriate. The next few pages feature recipes for luscious desserts made with cheese when just a piece of cheese won't do.

Baked Nut-crusted Camembert

Any thin-rind creamy cheese can be served this way.

1/2 cup chopped pecans or walnuts
1 1/2-pound-round (or oval) Camembert cheese
1 egg
Apple or pear slices
Sliced and lightly toasted rich bread such as brioche,
  panettone, or raisin pumpernickel

Preheat the oven to 350° F.

Place the nuts in a small ovenproof pan and toast in
the oven, stirring frequently, until lightly browned,
about 12 to 15 minutes. Remove from the oven and
cool, then chop and reserve.

Cut off and discard the top rind of the Camembert.
Beat the egg in a shallow container and place the cheese
in it. Turn the cheese to coat it on all sides with the
egg. Spread the nuts in a second shallow container and
transfer the Camembert to that container. Turning the
cheese, press the nuts onto all sides, to cover
completely. Place the cheese on a plate, cut side up,
cover, and chill for about 1 hour.

Increase the oven to 400° F.

Place the cheese on a cold baking sheet and bake until
the interior of the cheese is warm and runny, about 15
minutes. Transfer to a serving plate, surround with
fruit and bread slices, and serve piping hot.

Serves 8.

Boucheron in Phyllo

10 sheets (about 1/2 pound) *phyllo* dough, thawed
  (in the refrigerator) if frozen
About 1/4 pound (1 stick) unsalted butter, melted
  and cooled
1 pound Boucheron or other creamy goat's milk
  cheese, sliced into 8 1/2-inch-thick slices
Sifted powdered sugar
Chilled fresh cherries, berries, or grapes

Place 1 sheet of *phyllo* on a flat work surface. Keep
remaining dough covered with a lightly dampened
towel to prevent it from drying out. With a wide pastry
brush, lightly brush sheet with cooled melted butter to
cover completely. Top *phyllo* sheet with a second sheet
and lightly brush it with butter. Repeat until 5 sheets
in all are used. Create a second stack of buttered sheets
in the same manner. With a sharp knife, cut each stack
into quarters and place a slice of Boucheron on top in
the center of each quarter. Bring one side of *phyllo* up
and over to cover the cheese and brush the top of the
dough with butter. Bring the remaining *phyllo* sides
up and over the cheese, overlapping and buttering
them as you go, until all sides of the *phyllo* have been
folded over the cheese. Repeat with the remaining
phyllo stacks. Place the *phyllo* packages, seam side
down and well spaced, on a baking sheet and
refrigerate until ready to bake; they can rest up to
several hours.

Preheat the oven to 400° F.

Bake the *phyllo* packages until golden brown, about
10 to 15 minutes. Remove from the oven, dust lightly
with powdered sugar, and serve hot with chilled
cherries, berries, or grapes.

Serves 8.

Brie in Wine Aspic

Scottie McKinney, the San Francisco caterer's caterer, originated this idea some years ago. The same technique can be used with any flat-surfaced, edible-rind cheese. All the decorations should be edible.

To serve this stunning dish as an appetizer instead of at the end of the meal, use a dry white wine and a splash of vodka or other clear spirits in place of the fruity wine. Teetotalers can flavor the aspic with apple juice or chicken stock.

1 envelope (1 tablespoon) unflavored gelatin
1 cup water
3/4 cup fruity white wine
1 11- to 14-inch-round Brie cheese, chilled, or 2
**   7-inch-round Brie cheeses, chilled**
Fresh herbs such as basil, chives, cilantro (coriander),
**   dill, tarragon, or thyme**
Vegetables such as baby spinach or chard leaves,
**   celery leaves, or tiny mild peppers**
Fresh berries, grapes, kumquats, or sliced fruits
Edible flowers such as borage, citrus, nasturtiums,
**   jasmine, roses, squash blossoms, violas, or**
**   violets from pesticide-free plants, well rinsed**
**   to remove dust and insects**

To make the aspic, combine gelatin and 1/2 cup water in a small saucepan and let stand until the gelatin is soft, about 5 minutes. Place over medium heat and stir until gelatin dissolves, about 2 minutes. Remove from the heat and add the remaining 1/2 cup water and the wine. Nest the pan in a bowl of ice or place in the refrigerator until aspic thickens to the consistency of honey, occasionally stirring gently to prevent air bubbles from developing.

Meanwhile, place the cheese (or cheeses) on a wire rack sitting on a shallow-rimmed tray. Position decorations—herbs, vegetables or fruits, and/or flowers of choice—on top of the cheese to determine desired pattern, then set them aside. Spoon or brush a thin layer of aspic over the top and sides of cheese as evenly as possible. When the aspic is slightly tacky, dip the decorations into the liquid aspic and place them on the Brie in the selected pattern. Refrigerate, uncovered, until the layer of aspic sets up, about 15 minutes.

Remove the cheese from the refrigerator and cover the top and sides with a second layer of aspic, coating the decorations as well. It may be necessary to repeat with several layers of aspic, chilling between each application, to cover the cheese and decorations completely. The aspic coating should be between 1/16 and 1/8 inch thick. When the final coat has been applied, invert a large bowl over the cheese, making sure that it will not touch it, and chill until serving time. The cheese is best when completed only a few hours before serving, although some herbs, vegetables, and flowers will hold up if decorated as long as 36 hours in advance of serving.

A large Brie serves about 20; a small Brie about 10.

NOTE: Should the aspic get too thick before completing the decoration, melt it over heat and chill again until the correct consistency. Leftover aspic, including drippings on tray, can be refrigerated in a covered container for several days and reheated to begin the process again.

Cappuccino Cheesecake

This variation of my favorite cheesecake is rich, with its layer of strong coffee flavor and a creamy topping. Sprinkle with sweetened ground chocolate or cinnamon as you would a cup of cappuccino. Make the day before serving; the cheesecake keeps well for up to three days.

CRUST

1-1/4 cups graham-cracker crumbs (about 12 graham crackers)
1/3 cup firmly packed brown sugar
1 teaspoon ground cinnamon
1/4 pound (1 stick) unsalted butter, melted

FILLING

1-1/2 pounds Cream cheese, at room temperature
4 eggs
1 cup sugar
1 teaspoon vanilla extract
1/2 cup instant espresso powder, preferably Medaglia d'Oro, or to taste
1/2 cup coffee-flavored liqueur (optional)

TOPPING

1 cup heavy cream
2 tablespoons sugar
1 tablespoon vanilla extract
Sweetened cocoa powder or ground cinnamon

To make the crust, combine the graham cracker crumbs, brown sugar, and cinnamon in a mixing bowl. Add the melted butter and blend well with a fork. With your fingertips, press the mixture into a 10-inch springform pan and refrigerate while preparing the filling.

Preheat the oven to 375° F.

To make the filling, place the cheese in a medium-sized bowl and beat with an electric mixer until fluffy. Add the eggs, one at a time, and beat until smooth after each addition. Beat in sugar, vanilla extract, espresso powder, and coffee-flavored liqueur. Pour the cheese mixture into the crust and bake until almost set in the center when touched, about 45 minutes. Do not overbake. Remove from the oven and cool. Refrigerate for 24 hours.

Just before serving, remove the cheesecake from the pan and transfer to a serving plate. In a chilled metal bowl, whip the heavy cream with the sugar and vanilla extract just until it holds its shape. Spread on top of the cheesecake and sprinkle with cocoa or cinnamon to taste.

Serves 12.

Cheesecake Squares
with Lemon Curd

Serve these easy-to-make, three-layer cookies as snacks or desserts.

LEMON CURD

2 cups sugar
2 eggs
Grated zest and juice of 2 lemons
3 tablespoons unsalted butter

CRUST

1-1/2 cups graham-cracker crumbs (about 12 graham
     crackers)
1/3 cup firmly packed light brown sugar
5 tablespoons unsalted butter, melted

FILLING

1-1/2 pounds Cream cheese, softened
3/4 cup sugar
2 tablespoons unbleached all-purpose flour
3 eggs
1-1/2 teaspoons vanilla extract

To make the lemon curd, place the sugar in a mixing bowl and add the eggs, one at a time, beating well after each addition. Stir in lemon zest and juice. Pour mixture into the top pan of a double boiler set over simmering water. Add the butter, 1 tablespoon at a time, stirring constantly until butter melts and mixture thickens and coats a metal spoon. Remove from the heat and cool completely before using.

Preheat the oven to 350° F.

To make the crust, combine the graham-cracker crumbs, brown sugar, and melted butter in a medium-sized bowl and mix with a fork until well blended. Distribute the crumb mixture evenly in the bottom of a lightly buttered 9- x 13-inch sheet-cake pan, patting with fingers to firm. Bake for 5 minutes, remove from the oven and cool; reserve.

To make the filling, combine the Cream cheese and sugar in a large bowl and beat with an electric mixer until smooth and creamy. Beat in the flour until well blended. Add the eggs, one at a time, beating well after each addition. Stir in the vanilla extract. Pour over graham-cracker crust and bake until almost set, about 20 minutes. Turn off the heat, leave the oven door slightly ajar, and let cake cool in the oven for about 10 minutes. Remove from the oven and cool completely. When both cheese layer and lemon curd are completely cool, spread lemon curd evenly over cheese. Cover loosely and chill in the refrigerator for several hours.

With a knife blade that has been dipped in cold water, cut the chilled cheesecake into 2-inch squares and serve immediately, or store in the refrigerator for up to 3 days.

Makes 24 cookies.

Wine-poached Pears
Filled with Mascarpone
in Caramel Sauce

Mascarpone is a fresh triple-crème Italian cheese. If you cannot locate it, whipped softened Cream cheese is a meager alternative.

FILLING

1/2 cup Mascarpone cheese
1/4 cup powdered sugar, or to taste
2 to 3 tablespoons pear brandy

POACHED PEARS

Juice of 2 lemons
1 cup water
6 large ripe but firm pears, preferably Bosc
1/2 cup sugar
2 cups fruity white wine
Zest of 1 lemon, cut into thin strips
1 vanilla bean, split
1 3-inch cinnamon stick

CARAMEL SAUCE

1 cup heavy cream
3/4 cup sugar
1 cup water
1/4 cup pear brandy
3 tablespoons unsalted butter, at room temperature

Additional Mascarpone for garnish (optional)
Fresh mint leaves for garnish
Amaretti **(Italian almond cookies)**

To prepare the filling, combine the Mascarpone, powdered sugar, and pear brandy in a small bowl and whisk with a fork or wire whisk until well blended. Cover and refrigerate until needed.

To poach the pears, combine the lemon juice and water in a large bowl. Working with 1 pear at a time, peel as smoothly as possible, leaving stem intact. Cut a slice off the bottom of the pear so that it will stand upright. Core the pear from the bottom, and then immediately place it in the lemon juice and water bath to prevent discoloration while preparing the remaining pears.

Select a saucepan just large enough to later hold all the pears standing upright. Combine the sugar, wine, lemon zest, vanilla bean, and cinnamon stick in the saucepan. Bring the mixture to a boil over high heat, stirring to dissolve sugar.

Fill the pear cavities with crumpled foil. Stand the pears upright in the boiling poaching liquid, adding enough water to cover them. Reduce the heat so liquid simmers, cover the pan, and poach pears until they are tender but still hold their shape, 10 to 20 minutes. With a slotted spoon, carefully remove the pears to a shallow bowl and let cool.

When pears are cool, remove the crumpled foil from their cavities. Using a spoon or a pastry bag fitted with a medium-sized plain tip, fill pears with reserved Mascarpone filling. Stand pears upright on a tray or platter and chill until a few minutes before serving time.

To prepare the sauce, place the heavy cream in a small saucepan and scald over medium heat. Combine the sugar, water, and brandy in a small saucepan over moderate heat and cook, stirring, until the mixture is a caramel color. Remove from the heat. While continuously stirring, slowly add hot cream and then butter, and stir until butter melts. Keep the sauce warm.

To serve, place 1 pear on each dessert plate. Add a dollop of Mascarpone alongside pear. Slowly spoon warm sauce over the top of the pear, garnish with a mint leaf, and serve immediately with *amaretti.*

Serves 6.

Mascarpone and Fresh Fruit Ice Cream

The sublime combination of fresh fruit and creamy Mascarpone becomes pure nectar when turned into smooth ice cream. In the photograph, I've used mangoes; choose bananas, figs, nectarines, peaches, strawberries, raspberries, or other favorites. Strain berry purée through a sieve to remove seeds before mixing.

Minus the fruit, this rich ice cream was inspired by a recipe developed by Scottie McKinney using Fromage Blanc, a creamy fresh goat's milk cheese made in California by Laura Chenel, in place of the Mascarpone. If you can locate Fromage Blanc, I highly recommend using it, with or without my addition of figs. When neither Mascarpone nor Fromage Blanc is available, try whipped Cream cheese.

1 cup Mascarpone cheese or Fromage Blanc
1 cup heavy cream
4 egg yolks, beaten
1 cup sugar
1 cup puréed fresh fruit

Combine the cheese, heavy cream, egg yolks, sugar, and puréed figs and whisk to blend well. Freeze in an ice cream maker according to manufacturer's directions.

Serves 6.

Chocolate Coeur à la Crème with Raspberry Sauce

Traditionally these little molded hearts are made of plain Cream cheese. Double chocolate adds a new twist. I use Neuchâtel chocolate Cream cheese, made in Pennsylvania and available in most supermarkets. If you can't find it, substitute regular Cream cheese and add melted semisweet chocolate to taste. Ceramic *coeur à la crème* molds, with holes for draining excess liquid from cheese, are available in gourmet cookware stores.

Ice water
1/2 pound Neuchâtel chocolate-flavored Cream cheese
1/2 cup powdered sugar
1-3/4 cups heavy cream
3 to 4 cups fresh or frozen raspberries
Sugar
Raspberry liqueur
6 ounces (6 squares) semisweet chocolate
Tiny pink roses or petals, from pesticide-free plants, rinsed and dried
Sugar or butter cookies

Soak 4 8-inch squares of cheesecloth in ice water to cover.

Place the chocolate-flavored cheese and powdered sugar in a food processor and blend until very light and fluffy. Alternatively, combine the cheese and sugar in a small bowl and beat with a wire whisk or electric mixer.

In a chilled metal bowl, whip 1 cup heavy cream with a wire whisk or chilled electric beaters just until it holds its shape. Add to cheese mixture and whisk gently until well blended.

Wring out the cheesecloth pieces thoroughly and use them to line 4 individual *coeur à la crème* molds; allow excess cloth to overhang edges of molds. Spoon the cheese mixture into molds, heaping it slightly. Fold ends of cloth over the top of the cheese. Set a rack inside a large pan and arrange molds on rack. Refrigerate until liquid drains from cheese, at least 6 hours or for up to 2 days.

To make the raspberry sauce, reserve a few whole berries for garnish and purée remainder in a blender or food processor, adding sugar and raspberry liqueur to taste. Pass through a sieve to remove seeds. Refrigerate until serving time.

To make the chocolate glaze, combine the chocolate and remaining 3/4 cup heavy cream in a small heavy saucepan over medium heat. Heat, stirring, until chocolate melts and mixture is smooth. Remove from the heat and let stand, without beating, until lukewarm.

Remove the cheese hearts from their molds by grasping the cheesecloth ends and gently lifting the molded cheeses out. Remove the cheesecloth and place the cheese hearts on a wire rack sitting on a tray. Keep refrigerated until chocolate glaze is ready to use.

Spoon the chocolate glaze over chilled molded cheeses, spreading gently with a small spatula or brush. (Should the chocolate glaze get too thick, add a little bit of boiling water and stir to a smooth consistency.) Refrigerate for at least 30 minutes before serving; avoid chilling for more than a couple of hours to keep chocolate shiny.

To serve, ladle raspberry sauce onto individual plates. Place a chocolate cheese heart on top and garnish with reserved whole raspberries and roses or petals. Serve with sugar or butter cookies.

Serves 4.

Index

Recipe Index

ACKNOWLEDGMENTS

To Chronicle personnel, especially Drew Montgomery for suggesting that I do this book in the first place.

To Christine Conn, Maggie Cotton, Scottie McKinney, Lucille McNair, and Kristi Spence for sharing recipes.

To Phil Quattrociocchi and San Francisco International Cheese Imports, Inc. for providing many of the cheeses in the photographs, for securing cheeses for recipe testing and photography, and for sharing cheese information through the years.

To Burt Tessler and Jim Wentworth of Dishes Delmar for supplying the dinnerware shown throughout the book.

To Sue Fisher King, San Francisco, for supplying many of the table linens.

To Patricia Brabant for her stunning photography and bubbly enthusiasm that makes work such fun, and to Louis Block for his able assistance with the photography. Thanks also to Nelson Brabant for his valuable help in the studio.

To my sister Martha McNair for her valuable assistance in the studio.

To CTA Graphics, especially to Cleve Gallat for turning manuscript into type and Peter Linato for turning my layouts into pages.

To my supportive friends, especially John Carr and Gene Davis for their help and encouragement during the writing and photographing, and to Bob and Kristi Spence for luring me away from my work at the Lake Tahoe Rockpile in such a delightful way.

To world-class cheese tasters Addie Prey, Buster Booroo, Joshua J. Chew, and Michael T. Wigglebutt. Their tail-wagging compliments make my cooking worthwhile.

To my partner Lin Cotton for always being the big cheese in my life.